FUTUREWORLD

TOMORROW'S TECHNOLOGY TODAY

JOEL LEVY

CARLTON KiDS

CONTENTS

INTRODUCTION

The seeds of the future are here in the present. Today, in laboratories, factories and workshops, in computer simulations and on drawing boards, a huge range of mind-blowing technology is taking shape. Right now, someone is testing a flying motorcycle or a revolutionary material that will turn your clothes into solar cells. Lab technicians are growing replacement body parts for a patient, while others are fitting someone with a bionic foot. A researcher is working out how much faster than the speed of sound a magnetically levitating train will travel, even while a scientist in another laboratory is connecting a computer to someone's brain so that they can control a robotic arm in the next room by thought alone.

What's more, according to some **futurists** (people who try to predict the future), new technologies and inventions will arrive faster and faster as the pace of change accelerates, so that the next 50–60 years will see more technological progress than the previous 20,000 years combined.

But **FUTUREWORLD** is not science fiction. Everything in these pages either already exists or could, in theory, be achieved with current technology, with the possible exception of artificial intelligence (see page 10) and the space elevator (see page 69).

Secondly, **FUTUREWORLD** is about the near future, not the far future. While it covers projects that are being planned now but won't be completed until the far future, such as asteroid mining, this book mostly predicts developments that are likely to come to fruition over the next 15–25 years.

There are very good reasons for not looking too far ahead. As the Nobel Prize-winning nuclear physicist Niels Bohr once said: "Prediction is very difficult, especially about the future." Many previous attempts to predict the future have turned out to be wrong. In the 1960s, for instance, there was great excitement about the coming of personal jetpacks and free energy from nuclear fusion. Neither of these predictions has come true, and in fact the same joke is made about a lot of these technologies: they are twenty years away and always will be. Still, you can see the current developments in nuclear fusion on pages 36–37.

Futurists have also missed some of the biggest game changers. Few people in the 1960s would have predicted the impact of the internet on everyday life in the early 21st century, or that the biggest use for mobile phones would be texting rather than making video calls.

So which of the technologies in this book is most likely to make a big difference to you personally over the next few decades? The future tech that will change your life is most likely to be low cost, and involve existing technology that has already been proven.

This rules out, for instance, personal robot assistants, which, in order to work properly, will need some form of artificial intelligence – a technology that simply doesn't work yet. For most people it also rules out flying cars, which are already available (see page 50) but are likely to remain very expensive.

The most likely 'game-changer' is augmented reality (see page 22), which will cost no more than a pair of hi-tech sunglasses and could already be realized with existing computer power, yet has the potential literally to change the way that everyone sees the world.

Read the whole book and then decide for yourself – which of these technologies, from fuel cells to test-tube hamburgers, from kite power to flying robots, will have the biggest impact on your future world?

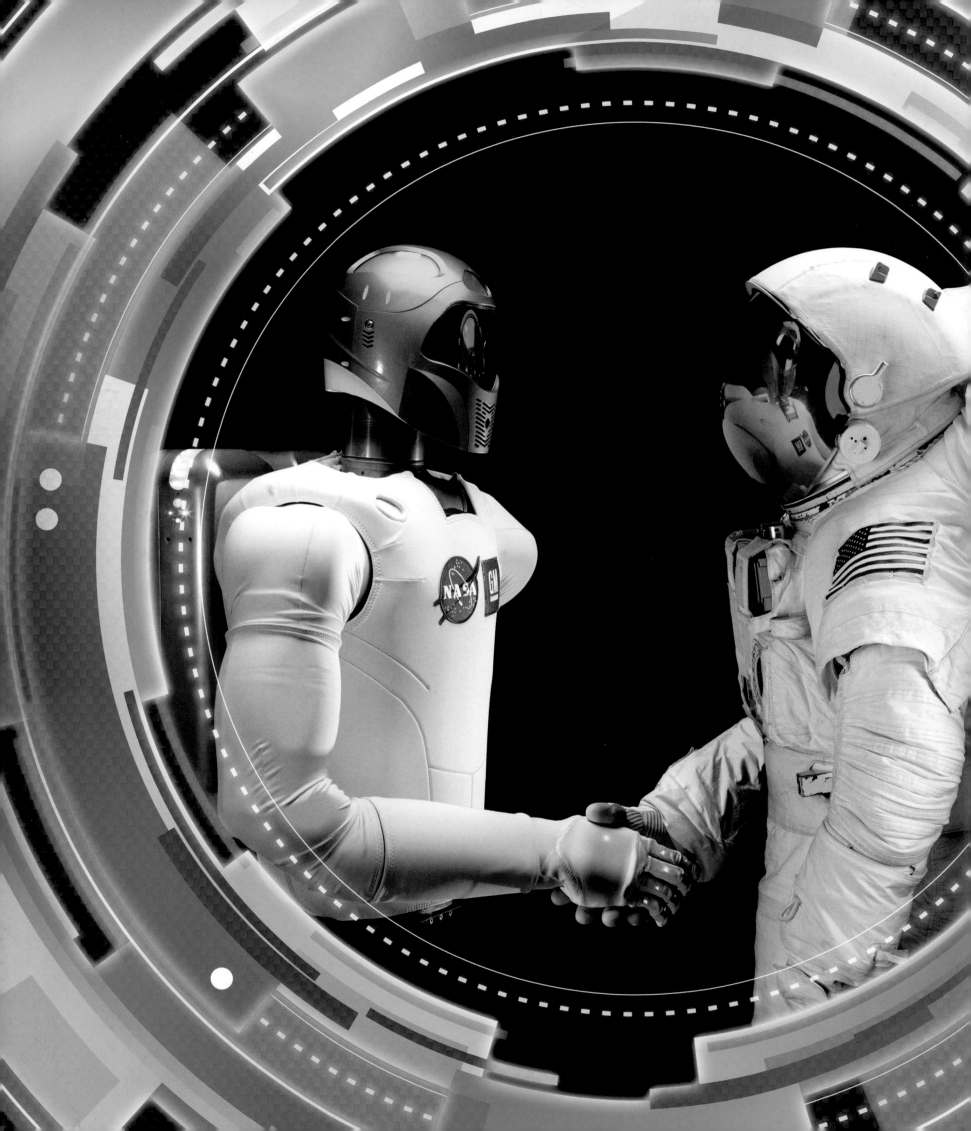

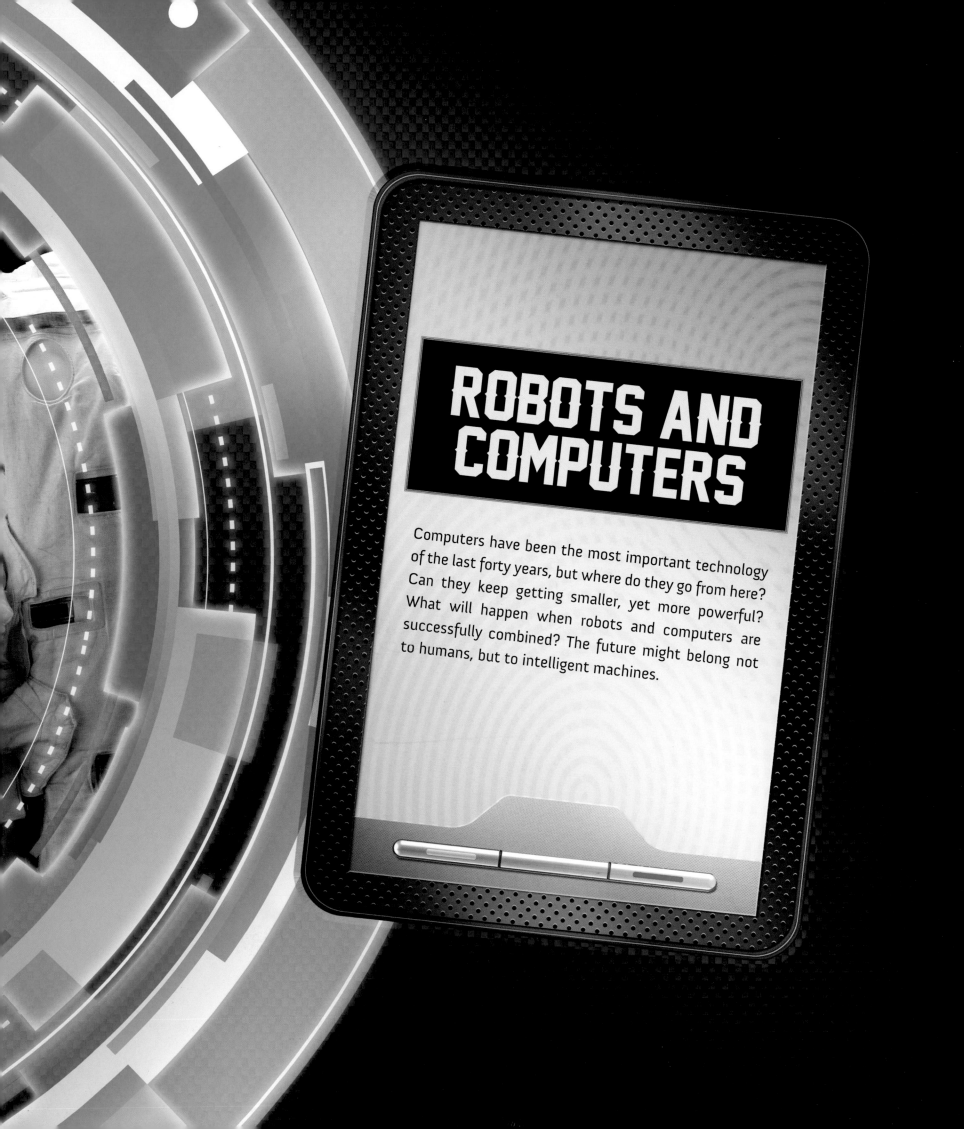

ROBOTS AND COMPUTERS

Computers have been the most important technology of the last forty years, but where do they go from here? Can they keep getting smaller, yet more powerful? What will happen when robots and computers are successfully combined? The future might belong not to humans, but to intelligent machines.

VIRTUALLY THERE
TELEPRESENCE

Telepresence ("distant presence") means being able to interact with faraway people and objects as if they were right here. Today's technology uses video screens that can turn or move around a bit, but in the near future it may be possible to remotely inhabit a robot that can walk, talk, touch and feel. Controlling a robot from a distance is called **telerobotics**.

RIGHT..
THE CURIOSITY ROVER IS REMOTE CONTROLLED FROM EARTH AS IT EXPLORES MARS.

ABOVE..
TELEMEDICINE LETS DOCTORS DIAGNOSE
PATIENTS THOUSANDS OF MILES AWAY.

GET CONNECTED

The main driving force behind the coming telepresence
revolution is **bandwidth** – the amount of information that
can be carried by a communication channel such as fibre-
optic cable or radio signal.

In the recent past the bandwidth available to individuals was
only enough for voice calls, but it will soon be possible for
anyone with a mobile phone/internet connection to send and
receive high-quality 3D images.

Robotic tools are becoming cheaper. Mobile cradles for smart
phones are already available, so that the screen showing your
face can turn around and even move from room to room.
In the near future your video presence will be able to walk
around and pick things up, thanks to telerobotic technology.

ABOVE..............................
A RESEARCHER TESTS A
ROBOTIC ARM CONTROLLED
BY BRAIN WAVES.

BELOW.................................
A JAPANESE EMERGENCY
ROBOT, DESIGNED TO WORK
IN DANGEROUS PLACES.

INTELLIGENT MACHINES
ARTIFICIAL INTELLIGENCE

Artificial intelligence (AI) is the ability of a machine to think, and not just follow a program. At the moment, machines can be programmed to do quite complex jobs, but only within limits. Tasks that humans find simple, such as navigating a crowded room or telling the difference between a weed and a flower, are too difficult for robots— so far.

AI IN OUR TIME

Films like *The Terminator*, *The Matrix* and *2001: A Space Odyssey* feature intelligent machines that have run out of control. In real life, however, AI cannot pilot spaceships or plot against humanity. The best-known real-world example of AI is probably Deep Blue, the chess-playing supercomputer that beat the world chess champion in 1997, but Deep Blue could not do anything except play chess.

More useful real-world examples of AI include computer programs that can write simple newspaper articles, and programs that control trillions of dollars of business deals without any help from humans. The Curiosity rover that is now exploring Mars uses a very limited form of AI to help it get around without banging into things or tipping over. Robonaut 2 (see right) has already been in use on the **International Space Station**.

ALL-SEEING EYES

If computer programs could be made intelligent enough to see like we do, computers could take over all sorts of important but boring and difficult jobs. In the next ten years, expect to see computers looking for criminals by spotting their faces on CCTV, or watching out for forest fires and dangerous weather events.

ABOVE..
ROBONAUT 2 IS DESIGNED TO WORK IN SPACE, USING THE SAME TOOLS AS HUMANS.

RIGHT..
THE MACGYVER PROJECT IS WORKING ON A RESCUE ROBOT FOR DISASTER SITUATIONS.

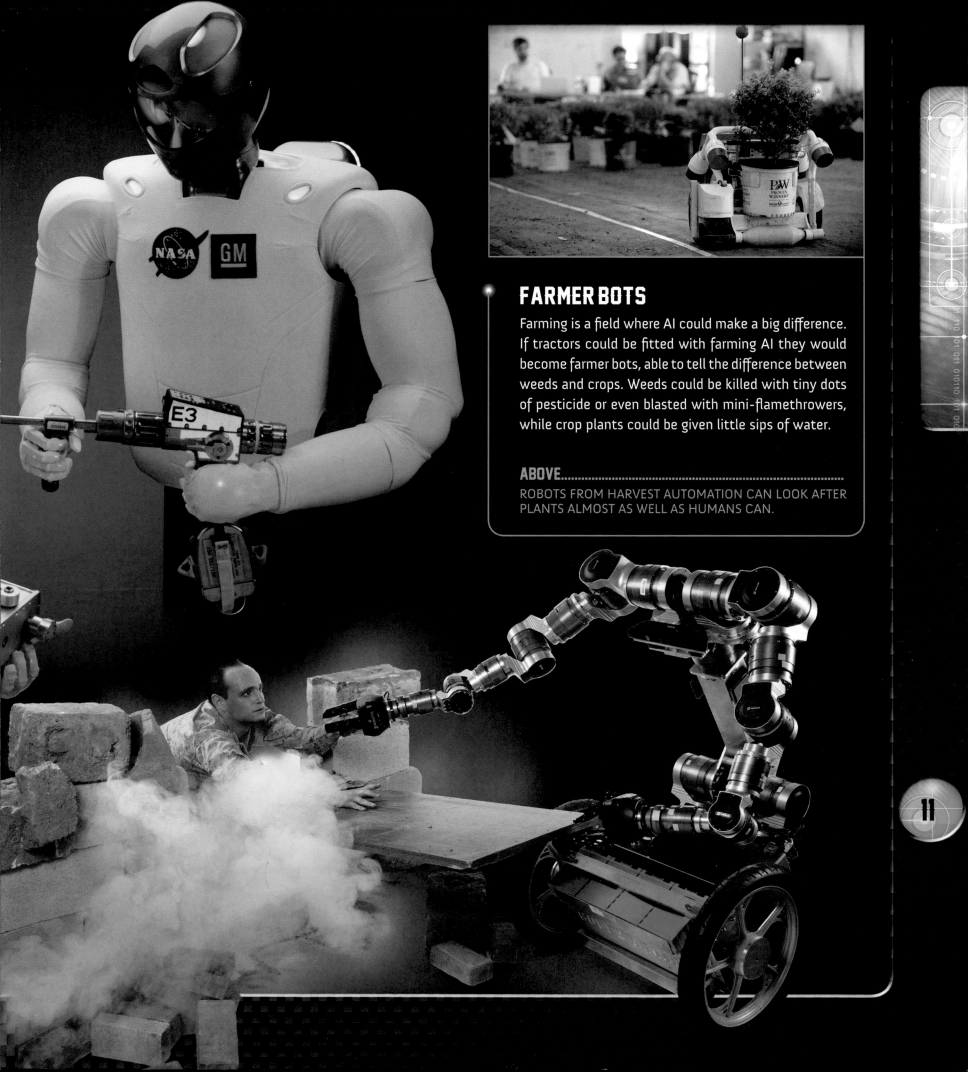

FARMER BOTS

Farming is a field where AI could make a big difference. If tractors could be fitted with farming AI they would become farmer bots, able to tell the difference between weeds and crops. Weeds could be killed with tiny dots of pesticide or even blasted with mini-flamethrowers, while crop plants could be given little sips of water.

ABOVE...
ROBOTS FROM HARVEST AUTOMATION CAN LOOK AFTER PLANTS ALMOST AS WELL AS HUMANS CAN.

POWER SUITS
EXOSKELETONS AND CARING ROBOTS

Exoskeleton means "outside skeleton". Animals like crabs and insects have exoskeletons. Thanks to exciting new technology, humans too can already benefit from exoskeletal "**power suits**", made of metal, carbon fibre and other strong, light materials. They boost the wearer's strength and endurance.

EARLY PROTOTYPES

To work properly the exoskeleton needs to be strong but light; it must move only when the user moves, and it must be able to carry its own power source. Early exoskeletons were too heavy and had to be plugged into the wall for their power.

EXOSKELETONS TODAY

Carbon fibre composites and advanced batteries mean that useful exoskeletons are already available. For instance, the HAL robotic suit from Cyberdyne (left) can be used by emergency workers, giving them extra power to move debris and lift injured people. NASA is developing the X1 exoskeleton for astronauts to wear, so that they can move heavy objects in space.

ABOVE LEFT...
THE HAL SUIT GIVES EMERGENCY WORKERS EXTRA LIFTING POWER.

SUPER-POWERS FOR EVERYONE

In the near future more advanced exoskeletons could become common in the military, helping soldiers to carry heavy loads on long marches; in healthcare, making it easier for nurses to lift patients; and for the disabled, helping paralysed people to walk.

In the more distant future power suits could become relatively common, so that workers in factories and warehouses would be able to lift heavy items, astronauts visiting Jupiter would be able to cope with high gravity, and even ordinary people could run faster, jump higher, lift more and enjoy super-powers similar to Iron Man.

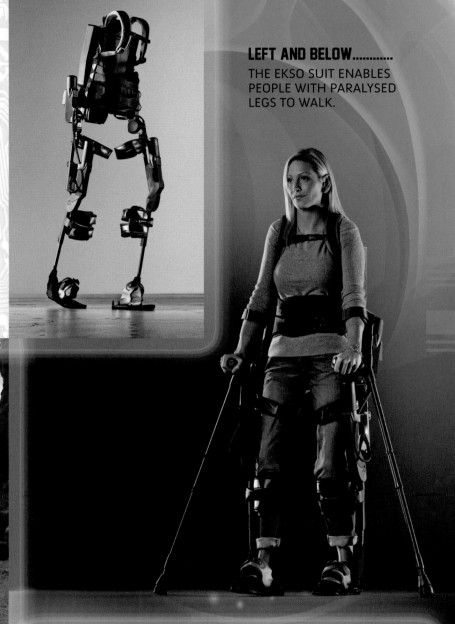

LEFT AND BELOW.............
THE EKSO SUIT ENABLES PEOPLE WITH PARALYSED LEGS TO WALK.

ABOVE...
THE FRENCH-DESIGNED HERCULE ROBOT HELPS HUMANS TO CARRY HEAVY LOADS.

LEFT...
THE X1 ROBOTIC EXOSKELETON WILL HELP ASTRONAUTS MOVE OBJECTS IN SPACE.

CARING ROBOTS

Caring robots are robotic nurses and companions that can lift elderly or ill people, help them get about, keep them company and even help with shopping, cooking and other day-to-day tasks.

Caring robots already available include ROBOHELPER, which helps people get out of bed, the Robovie, which carries shopping, and Toyota's Human Support Robot, which can pick up objects and relay video calls. In the near future robot pets will provide companionship for elderly people living alone, while at the same time monitoring their health and helping them out around the house.

SQUEEZABLE CIRCUITRY
THE COMPUTERS OF TOMORROW

The first computers were giant machines that filled entire rooms and took a whole day to do a single sum. Yet today a small games console packs as much power as a 1997 supercomputer.

MOORE'S LAW

Since the late 1970s computers have followed a rule set out by leading computer engineer Gordon Moore. He predicted that the number of **transistors** that could be crammed onto a single **chip** would double every two years. More transistors = more computing power, so Moore was effectively saying that computers would double in power every two years. Amazingly, he was right. In 1969 the computer that guided the Apollo spaceship to the Moon had around 17,000 transistors; today your desktop computer has up to 14 billion transistors on a chip.

So will computers in 2025 be 64 times as powerful as they were in 2013? Possibly. Scientists have long predicted that Moore's law will run up against the limits of physics — for instance, if transistors are too tiny they become invisible to the electrons that make them work. But breakthroughs with carbon nanotubes (a form of **nanotechnology**) suggest that Moore's law will hold true for a while longer.

ABOVE..............................
FUTURE QUANTUM COMPUTERS MAY HAVE CRYSTALS AT THEIR CORE.

RIGHT...................................
THE INSIDE OF AN EXPERIMENTAL QUANTUM COMPUTER MADE BY D-WAVE.

QUANTUM COMPUTING

According to quantum physics, some **subatomic particles** can be in more than one place at once, so they can carry out more than one calculation at a time. If crystal-based computers could harness this ability they could become thousands of times more powerful. At the moment, however, even the simplest **quantum computers** involve high-power lasers, superconductors cooled with liquid nitrogen and other expensive and difficult technology.

RIGHT....................................
HANDS-FREE TABLETS
ARE CURRENTLY UNDER
DEVELOPMENT, USING EYE-
TRACKING TECHNOLOGY.

BELOW....................................
THE MOTOROLA HC-1 IS A
HANDS-FREE COMPUTER
THAT RESPONDS TO VOICE
COMMANDS.

COMPUTERS YOU CAN SQUEEZE

The touchscreen is already replacing the keyboard, and voice and gesture control of computers are also available. These will become more widespread, as will other ways of communicating with your computer.

For instance, you might be able to make something with modelling clay that is wired up to a computer, which in turn will be able to make physical versions of virtual objects for you to play with and mould. Foldable screens will become available, and it will be possible to make a computer out of almost any material.

15

RIGHT....................................
WITH SANDSCAPE YOU COULD SHAPE AN OBJECT
FROM SAND AND SEE IT APPEAR ON SCREEN.
BEFORE IT IS MANUFACTURED FOR REAL.

ROBO-BEASTS
BIOMIMETIC ROBOTS

Science fiction has been predicting robots for 100 years, yet the only ones you are likely to see today are factory production robots, or expensive little discs that vacuum the floor (very slowly). It has turned out to be incredibly hard to make robots that can look after themselves and do something useful.

But what if nature had the answer? An exciting new field in robotics looks at animals for inspiration, creating robots which are **biomimetic**: they mimic biology.

BETTER BY DESIGN

Why should nature be a good model for robots? There is a sort of design process at work in nature: evolution. Fish can swim more efficiently than any submarine; insects can fly further using less energy than any drone; and mammals can run up rocky mountain slopes that no vehicle can cope with. By looking at how animals achieve these feats, roboticists can design robo-creatures that share some of their abilities.

ABOVE
AQUAPENGUINS CAN SWIM ON THEIR OWN AND COMMUNICATE WITH EACH OTHER USING SONAR.

ROBOT CREATURES

Energy efficiency is one of the biggest problems facing robots, which have to carry heavy batteries and need to squeeze every last ounce of power from them. One way of getting around this is to learn from the tricks used by living creatures.

AquaPenguin copies the swimming style of the penguin to save energy while swimming. Robots like these could soon be used for water monitoring in harbours and out in the ocean.

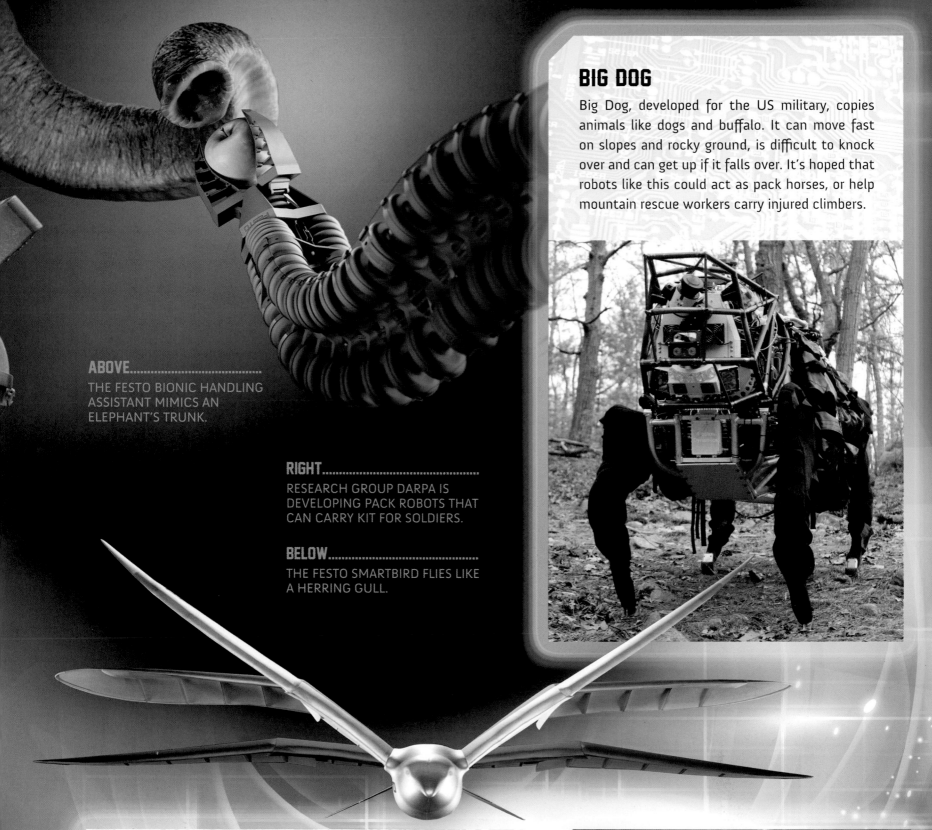

BIG DOG

Big Dog, developed for the US military, copies animals like dogs and buffalo. It can move fast on slopes and rocky ground, is difficult to knock over and can get up if it falls over. It's hoped that robots like this could act as pack horses, or help mountain rescue workers carry injured climbers.

ABOVE......................................

THE FESTO BIONIC HANDLING ASSISTANT MIMICS AN ELEPHANT'S TRUNK.

RIGHT......................................

RESEARCH GROUP DARPA IS DEVELOPING PACK ROBOTS THAT CAN CARRY KIT FOR SOLDIERS.

BELOW......................................

THE FESTO SMARTBIRD FLIES LIKE A HERRING GULL.

FLIGHT AND SPEED

Robotic bees and dragonflies need little energy for flying because they are very light. By flying in the same way as their insect inspirations do, they can hover, land and take off vertically and be highly manoeuvrable. Such robo-critters could be used for surveillance, or to explore buildings damaged by fire or earthquake.

RIGHT......................................

ANOTHER DARPA ROBOT, THE CHEETAH, CAN RUN AT 29MPH.

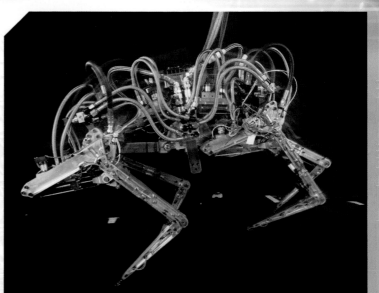

17

SHOPPING AND LIFESTYLE

The greatest impact of technology for most people comes in their day-to-day lives, in ways that are often almost invisible. Did you know, for instance, that many of the things you buy today – even clothes and packets of food – contain tiny microchips that talk to computer control systems?

This section explores the ways in which everyday life could change in the near future. Learn how your smartphone will take over your life and disappear at the same time; how your fridge will order your groceries for you; and how your friends could lleave digital graffiti visible only to you.

SMART MONEY
FUTURE SHOPPING

Ten years from now, shopping will be very different. As you walk past a shop it will offer you a special deal on exactly what you want. You will walk in, pick up the goods and walk out without going through checkout or handing over any money.

SMART SHOPPING

The internet has already caused big changes in shopping – for instance, there are very few record shops anymore because music is increasingly downloaded on-line. Smartphones are also beginning to affect the way people shop; it is now common for shoppers to find an item they like in a physical shop and then use their smartphone to see if it is cheaper online or somewhere else.

NEAR-FIELD COMMUNICATION

Many items now carry microchips called **radio frequency identification** (RFID) tags, which are able to broadcast simple information about the item, such as its serial number and price. These can be monitored by scanners and by some new smartphones, and RFID tags are already used as security devices and to help shops work out what has been bought and needs replacing, automatically. RFID tags in adverts or even magazines can also signal to your smartphone to pass on offers, adverts and information.

Over the next 5–10 years, RFID technology will be replaced with a similar but more advanced version called **near-field communication** (NFC). With RFID, tags can signal to smartphones, but the "conversation" is one way. In NFC, the conversation is two-way; slightly more advanced versions of RFID tags give items, adverts and even walls, counters, bags and boxes the ability to "talk" to your smartphone. Provided the phone and the tag come within ten centimetres of one another, they can exchange information. For instance, if you see an advert for a movie you want to see, you could put your phone next to it and book tickets then and there. To pay for an item, you simply need to touch your phone to the cash register, or possibly even just to the item itself.

Eventually, when wireless communication between smartphones and the internet is always on, everywhere, you and your electronic wallet will be tracked, and your smartphone will automatically register what you have picked up. A shopping trip might involve simply walking into the shop, picking up whatever you want and leaving; the payment will be automatically taken out of your bank account.

StyleMe™

VIRTUAL REFLECTIONS

More visible technology will include virtual mirrors, which can show you not just your reflection but what you would look like wearing the clothes you have just picked up. While you look in the mirror, a shopping assistant robot may be holding your bags for you.

ABOVE..
THE STYLEME ELECTRONIC MIRROR MAKES TRYING ON CLOTHES IN A SHOP EASY.

BELOW...
SMARTPHONES COULD SOON BE THE STANDARD WAY TO PAY FOR A MEAL IN A RESTAURANT.

3D PRINTING

Perhaps the greatest advance in shopping will be 3D printing. At the moment a 3D printer is a device that uses liquid plastic to print a 2D layer, just like an inkjet printer. The plastic quickly sets hard, and then the printer prints another layer on top of it, building up the layers until a three-dimensional product is formed. Already there are printers that can use other materials, such as wood and metal, and 3D printers can make things with moving parts and **electronic** components. By 2025 you may not need to go to the shops at all: you will simply choose a product on line, hit "print", and your own personal version will be printed out for you at home.

ABOVE..
THE MAKERBOT REPLICATOR CREATES PROFESSIONAL-STANDARD PLASTIC MODELS.

A NEW WAY OF SEEING
AUGMENTED REALITY

If you look at a picture of the Roman Coliseum online, you can see notes, links to extra information, and even recreations of what it used to look like.

Imagine if you could see all these things while actually in the Coliseum, so that when you looked at the ruined floor of the arena you could see, superimposed on top of it, a recreation of what it once looked like, with gladiators battling against a backdrop of baying crowds. Thanks to Augmented Reality (AR), this is already possible.

RIGHT...
IMAGINE VISITING A DINOSAUR THEME PARK! WEARING AR GLASSES, YOU COULD WALK AROUND THE PARK AND SEE IMAGES OF EXTINCT CREATURES, ALONG WITH TEXT INFORMATION.

BELOW...................................
GOOGLE SMART-GLASSES CONTAIN A COMPUTER THAT PROJECTS DATA ONTO THE LENS.

SMART GLASSES AND HUDS

Augmented means 'improved' or 'added to'. **Augmented Reality** means information and/or images electronically added to the real world, which you can see in real time at real locations.

So far you can only see AR by looking at a scene through a smartphone or tablet, but Google's Project Glass smart-glasses showcase technology that will soon become widespread. Smart-glasses project info and visuals onto the lenses of the glasses, which are transparent enough to look through and see the real world. Versions of this technology have long been a feature of **head-up displays** (HUDs) for fighter-pilots, where navigation and radar information are shown on the inside of the pilot's visor.

More advanced versions of smart-glasses are already emerging. For instance, the military is working on smart-glasses for soldiers that combine pictures from infra-red and night vision cameras with what the soldier can already see, so that he or she can effectively see in the dark. Skiers, snowboarders and base jumpers can now buy goggles with HUD-style technology to display GPS info.

DIGITAL GRAFFITI AND VIRTUAL FAMILIARS

Almost every aspect of life could be touched by AR. When you are shopping, AR will bring up the prices and available sizes and colours of items as soon as you look at them. You could look at an advert and directions to the relevant store would pop up. If a friend wanted to warn you that a restaurant had bad food, she could leave **digital graffiti**: a virtual message embedded in cyberspace, which you would see in AR when you looked at the restaurant.

You could generate virtual characters, creatures and scenes that you would encounter through AR, or you could be accompanied by your own virtual **"familiar"** – imagine a small dragon that only you can see, which acts as a digital assistant.

AUGMENTED INFORMATION

AR is already used in tourism. Imagine how exciting historical sites could be if you could see a recreation virtually overlaid on the scene, or museums if you could look at a skeleton and see a virtual recreation of the animal superimposed on top of it.

At school or college, AR could add background information to a picture posted by the teacher, or let you look up answers on the internet with just a glance.

ABOVE..

AR ALLOWS A TOURIST TO WALK DOWN A STREET AND SEE IMAGES OF HOW IT USED TO BE ON HIS IPAD.

Tyrannosaurus Rex
A fearsome predator that walked the Earth 66 million years ago.

23

SUPERCOMPUTER IN YOUR POCKET
FUTURE SMARTPHONES

The smartphone in your pocket is already more powerful than a desktop computer from two or three years ago, but if you use a computer for work or school the chances are you still find yourself sat at a desk with a desktop or laptop computer.

The actual processing part of the computer may have shrunk to pocket-size, but there is still no substitute for a proper keyboard and a decent-sized screen. These are the things that still tie us to desktop devices. But all that may be about to change, and the smartphone will soon be set free to take over your digital life.

DEVICE CONVERGENCE

Smartphones already have the processing power to handle documents, play video and surf the net, and they already display something called **device convergence**. This is where jobs that used to need different devices can all be done by a single device.

Previously you needed a camera to take pictures, because cameras could handle film, while you needed a CD player to play music, because music was on CDs. Now, though, your smartphone includes phone, camera, computer, stereo, web browser and sat-nav. Nissan have developed an app that allows a smartphone to drive a car, and there are apps for controlling the heating in your home, monitoring house alarms, checking your health and listening out for restless babies. Soon smartphones will take over the jobs of credit card and wallet (see page 20), door and car keys, passport, travel passes and airline tickets.

It will be more accurate to describe your smartphone as a **personal digital assistant** (PDA). What's more, the PDA device could play host to a virtual assistant, an artificial intelligence that anticipates your needs and does routine tasks for you such as booking flights or "talking" to your fridge to see if it needs to order milk. Google Now and Apple's Siri are primitive versions of this.

BELOW..
THE MEMOTO LIFEBLOGGING CAMERA IS A FORERUNNER
OF THE ALWAYS-ON PDA. IT TAKES TWO PHOTOS A MINUTE,
CREATING A COMPLETE RECORD OF THE WEARER'S PAST.

EVOLVING PDAS

What about the need for screens and keyboards? Using near field communication (see page 20) and advanced wireless technology, and harnessing the processing muscle of cloud-based computing, your PDA will wirelessly plug into whatever devices are nearby. Since it will soon be possible for almost any surface in the house, school or car to double as a screen, there will be no shortage of screens available. You won't need a keyboard or mouse because you will be able to control the PDA by voice or gesture.

What will your PDA look like? Miniaturisation, cloud-based computing power and new materials mean your future smartphone could look like almost anything, or even flit from item to item, "possessing" whatever was nearby. You could even have a malleable phone like a lump of clay or one that scrunches up and unfolds when you need it.

ABOVE...................................
NOKIA ARE DEVELOPING
THE MORPH, A BENDY
PHONE WHICH YOU CAN
WEAR AROUND YOUR
WRIST.

25

INTELLIGENT LIVING
SMART HOMES AND SCHOOLS

BELOW...
THE DIGITAL CHOCOLATIER
CREATES CUSTOM CHOCOLATES.

Over the next decade, clever technology will save you energy, taking care of all the most boring jobs, making you comfortable and educating you. Digital technology will be built into the fabric of houses, so that computers can control every aspect of the home and talk to you wherever you are.

Using printable foodstuffs such as lab-grown meat proteins, your food printer will be able to create everything from burgers and burritos to weird and wonderful new taste sensations.

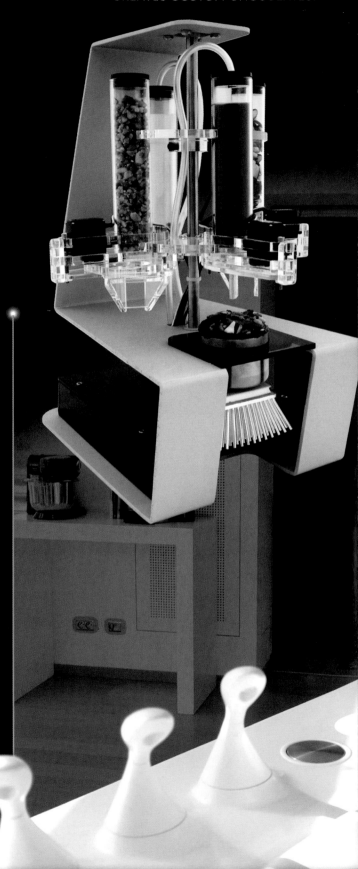

ELECTRICITY EVERYWHERE

Buildings of the future won't have plug sockets. Induction technology will make it possible to charge phones, robots and other technology without wires. To save energy, computers controlling appliances will automatically shut down anything that is not in use.

Your smart home will be able to welcome guests and block intruders by using **biometric scanning** to confirm identity. It will be able to read your face, understand your voice commands and recognize your gestures so that you can tell it what to do or simply let it look after you. It might spot that you are feeling gloomy and choose one of your favourite songs to cheer you up.

Robots will feature in your future home, but they will be small and slow and putter about in the background, doing the boring housework. Some will be able to climb walls or fly around, so they can reach those cobwebby corners. Sensing your movements, they will stay out of your way.

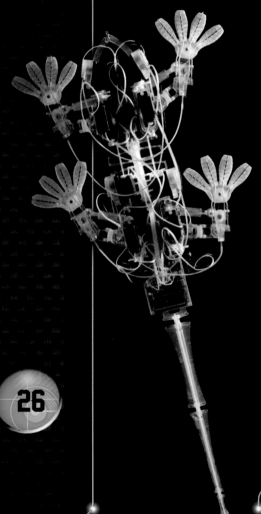

ABOVE LEFT..
STICKYBOT, A GECKO-INSPIRED
CLIMBING ROBOT. THE HOUSE
CLEANER OF THE FUTURE?

BELOW..................................
THIS AMAZING FUTURISTIC
FRIDGE STORES AND COOLS
FOOD BY SUSPENDING IT IN
BIOPOLYMER GEL

VIRTUAL EDUCATION

The school of the future might not be a physical school at all. Online education is taking off, with millions of students already receiving tuition over the internet, watching lessons/lectures on web videos, submitting coursework by email, taking part in tuition groups and seminars by live chat sessions and having personal education tailored to their individual needs. Over the next twenty years a bigger proportion of education will be done via the internet, and students will graduate from top universities without ever having been in the same country as their lecturers.

The schools that remain might look slightly different. Whiteboards will be replaced by interactive glass screens, linked to tablets in every student's hand or as part of their desks. You won't have to go up to the board to complete an exercise, because what you write on your screen will appear at the front of the class. Students will access textbooks via their computers and upload and download homework this way too. Teachers themselves might be replaced by robots – a recent experiment in Japan showed that children enjoyed learning English by interacting with a teaching robot programmed to be less able than they were, so that they learned by teaching it.

ABOVE..
TOUCH-SENSITIVE GLASS SCREENS COULD
REPLACE WHITEBOARDS IN SCHOOLS.

27

LEFT..
THE HOUSE OF THE FUTURE WILL HAVE A
KITCHEN RANGE MADE OF INTERACTIVE GLASS.

WEARABLE TECHNOLOGY
INTELLIGENT CLOTHING

Suppose your jacket could sense the weather and change from keeping you warm to cooling you down? What if your trousers turned the energy you burn when walking into power to charge your smartphone? Wouldn't it be useful if your swimsuit or skiwear included technology to keep you safe and signal to rescuers in an emergency?

All these scenarios could come true withiin the next 15 years thanks to smart fabrics.

LEFT.............................
THE NIKE FUELBAND MEASURES HOW ACTIVE YOU ARE.

WEARABLE ELECTRONICS

Intelligent clothing is made from new or yet-to-be-invented materials, which can change the way we think about clothes. Thanks to nanotechnology it is becoming possible to make strong, thin sheets of material that can transmit electronic signals, turn heat and light into electricity and vice versa, and which can be used as part of gizmos and gadgets.

Computers, keyboards and even screens can be built into fabrics, so that you can wear clothes that light up, convert motion and sunlight into electricity and even double as a computer display. New materials are being developed that are more resistant than ever to heat, cold, radiation and impacts.

UNDERWEAR THAT LOOKS AFTER YOU

Intelligent clothing will affect fashion, with the arrival of clothes that can be changed to suit your mood or location, or which can be programmed to display different patterns or images. Wearable electronics will make computers more portable than ever, and put your clothes to work.

It is already possible, for instance, to buy bras and vests that monitor heart rate, blood pressure and breast health. By the 2020s sophisticated health monitoring could be built in to underwear as standard.

RIGHT.......................................
THE FIRST WARNING SYSTEM SMART BRA CAN DETECT BREAST CANCER BEFORE DOCTORS DO.

SELF-MENDING FABRIC AND INVISIBILITY CLOAKS

One recently invented fabric not only conducts electricity but can heal itself if cut or torn. Clothes made from this would not only mend themselves, but would keep your gadgets connected all the time.

Also in prototype are so-called invisibility cloaks. These use **fibre optics** to direct light around the body, so that the cloak acts as a screen to project the scene beyond the wearer, masking his or her presence.

LEFT...
THIS SEE-THROUGH COAT FROM THE TACHI LAB IN JAPAN IS MADE OF OPTIC FIBRES THAT DIRECT LIGHT AROUND THE WEARER.

SURVIVAL SUITS

Perhaps the biggest difference will come in the field of extreme performance clothing, such as adventure sportswear, survival clothing, uniforms for emergency workers and even spacesuits. For instance, researchers at MIT have designed the BioSuit: a skin-tight spacesuit that is far less awkward than the traditional version. In the future they plan to include artificial muscles to create a kind of exoskeletal power suit (see page 12).

If relatively lightweight fabrics can resist the temperature and pressure extremes of space, suits for mountain climbers, deep sea divers and extreme snowboarders could become equally light and skin-tight, while still protecting against even the harshest weather. With built-in radio transmitters, such suits could also signal to rescuers in case of emergency. Skiers can already take advantage of airbag-style survival suits for avalanche protection; perhaps light and flexible impact-resistant fabrics will become a standard part of both extreme sportswear and emergency services uniforms.

LEFT..............................
INVENTOR PROFESSOR DAVA NEWMAN SHOWS OFF THE BIOSUIT.

VA...

Toda...
being...
proje...
tubes...
pump...
coole...
get v...
carry...
gene...
can b...

ET3...

The...
build...
and c...
6,50...
two...
with...
rails...
50 m...

BELOW...
TUBU...
WITH...

ENERGY, TRANSPORT AND THE ENVIRONMENT

The biggest problems facing the world over the next century relate to energy: how to get enough of it, how to use less of it, and how to make it without causing pollution.

Technological answers to all these problems are emerging from laboratories and moving out into the world, from green energy solutions that could convert endlessly renewable power sources into cheap electricity, to high-speed, eco-friendly transport options.

This chapter features updates on technologies from the past — such as sails, kites and airships — and ones that belong in the far future, such as lightcraft and nuclear fusion.

WILL ELECTROMAGNETIC MONORAILS BE
THE TRANSPORTATION OF THE FUTURE?

INSPIRATION FROM THE SUN
NUCLEAR FUSION

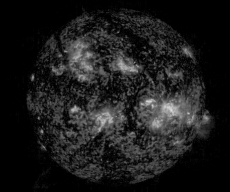

The Sun is powered by a process called **nuclear fusion**, which turns minuscule amounts of hot gas into colossal amounts of energy. If we could harness the same process here on Earth, we could generate masses of cheap energy with virtually no pollution.

$E=MC^2$

Fusion occurs when subatomic particles get squashed together so hard and at such high temperatures that they fuse or merge. The resulting particle is ever so slightly lighter (i.e. less massive) than the original ones, and as is expressed by Einstein's famous equation $e=mc^2$, a little bit of mass equals an enormous amount of energy. Fusion should not be confused with nuclear fission, which is where the nucleus of a radioactive atom like uranium splits apart. This also releases nuclear energy, although not quite as much, and it leaves behind extremely dangerous radioactive waste.

THE BREAK-EVEN CHALLENGE

Fusion power uses a form of hydrogen that is found in seawater, and produces no waste gases and virtually no radioactive waste. If it can be made to work, it can convert small amounts of cheap fuel into a huge supply of energy.

Unfortunately the technology of nuclear fusion is very hard to get right. The fuel must be heated and squashed to an unimaginable degree, and this takes huge amounts of energy. After 60 years of research scientists are still at least 20 years away from making useable fusion power, which will come when they can get more energy out of nuclear fusion than it takes to get it going — the break-even point.

ABOVE............................
THE INTERIOR OF GERMANY'S ASDEX (AXIALLY SYMMETRIC DIVERTOR EXPERIMENT) UPGRADE FUSION REACTOR.

RIGHT...................
TOKAMAK FUSION
TEST REACTOR
AT PRINCETON
UNIVERSITY, USA.

LASERS AND TOKOMAKS

At the moment two enormous projects and lots of smaller ones (pictured) are underway to reach the break-even point. At the National Ignition Facility in the US, 192 high-powered lasers are focused on a tiny pellet of fuel, causing it to explode into a ball of hot gas called a plasma. The shock waves from the explosion smash the plasma into a tiny point, and this is then heated with another laser blast so that it ignites – i.e. the fusion reaction begins.

Meanwhile in Europe a project called ITER is currently planning to build a fusion reactor in France. Here, plasma is heated up by blasting it with microwaves and beams of particles travelling at close to the speed of light, and then crushed by massive magnetic fields until fusion is achieved. This kind of reactor is called a **tokomak**.

Unfortunately the cost of ITER has now reached over 15 billion Euros and the completion date has been delayed until 2020, while the actual firing up of the reactor is not going to happen until 2027 at best. The plan is for ITER to prove that break-even is possible, and then to build an even bigger tokomak reactor called DEMO, which would be the first working fusion power plant, and the most expensive technological project ever.

RIGHT..
THE STELLARATOR WENDELSTEIN 7-X
NUCLEAR FUSION REACTOR, GERMANY.

GREEN POWER
SOLAR LOOP

The Solar Loop, proposed for Freshkills Park in New York, consists of two different surfaces that twist one into the other. The photovoltaic surface is always exposed to the sun, while the mirrored surface reflects light from the surrounding area. The shape of the structure allows it to follow the arc of the sun at at its best angle over the course of the day.

If the project goes ahead, the loop could be built on a small scale – the size of a pavilion – or on a huge scale, depending on budget.

THE SOLAR LOOP COULD BE
USED FOR CONCERTS AND
OTHER PUBLIC EVENTS.

BELOW......................................
ARTIST'S IMPRESSION OF THE
SOLAR LOOP IN THE SUNSHINE.

WORLD HACK
GEOENGINEERING

Geoengineering is the technology of changing natural systems by human actions. Global warming is almost certainly an example of unintentional geoengineering. Thanks to the billions of tonnes of carbon dioxide (CO_2) and other **greenhouse gases** pumped into the atmosphere by humans, the world is getting hotter. This is causing ice caps to melt, sea levels to rise and weather to change, with more and bigger storms and changes to seasonal weather patterns like the monsoon rains in India.

RIGHT...................................
A WORKER TENDS TO A POND OF ALGAE IN FRANCE.

BELOW...................................
AN ARTIST'S IMPRESSION OF SPACE MIRRORS IN ORBIT.

DIRECT ACTION

Worries about global warming have led to efforts to reduce the amount of greenhouse gas we produce, but these efforts have mostly failed, leading to suggestions that we need to tackle the greenhouse effect directly. Industrial-scale human activity caused the problem so maybe action on a similar scale could solve it.

This is where geoengineering comes in, with proposals that could directly remove CO^2 from the air, encourage plants to soak up more of it, or cool the atmosphere to counteract the greenhouse effect.

CARBON SCRUBBING AND FREEZING

One suggestion for removing CO_2 directly is to use **carbon scrubbers**. These use chemical "sponges" to soak up carbon from the air. On a small scale they are common in submarines and spaceships, but for geoengineering they would need to be as big as cities, with enormous fans and some way of removing the carbon from the sponges, which in turn would eat up vast amounts of energy.

OCEAN SEEDING

CO_2 is naturally removed from the atmosphere by plants; perhaps geoengineering could copy this approach?

Experiments have already taken place where iron filings were dumped into the ocean. The sea is full of tiny floating plants called algae and phytoplankton, but normally the growth of these is limited by a lack of available iron. Iron filings act like fertilizer, triggering massive blooms of ocean plants, which soak up loads of CO_2 from the air before dying and sinking to the bottom of the ocean, taking the carbon with them. Unfortunately these blooms also tend to be poisonous and bad for other ocean creatures.

AEROSOLS AND SPACE MIRRORS

If removing CO_2 is too difficult, perhaps geoengineering can take a tip from volcanoes. When a big volcano erupts, it blasts billions of tiny particles into the atmosphere, collectively known as an aerosol. Aerosols become the seeds for clouds of tiny water droplets, and because clouds are white they reflect light and heat from the Sun back out into space before it gets to Earth. A big volcanic eruption can cool down the Earth for years.

Humans could do something similar by creating artificial aerosols. One plan is for a fleet of ocean-going boats to pick up seawater and spray it into the atmosphere, or for teams of blimps to fly around spraying chemicals into the upper atmosphere. Science-fiction-style plans call for giant mirrors in space to stop sunlight getting to Earth, or for colossal guns to fire millions of ceramic discs into low orbit for the same reason.

All these approaches would probably cause catastrophic changes to global climate even if they worked. Simpler, easier and more eco-friendly options might include reforestation (planting trees) or simply painting our roofs white.

POWER PACKED
ELECTRICITY MOVES ON

What if the battery in your phone could last for months on a single charge, or a box the size of a microwave oven could power your home? This is the promise of fuel cell technology.

A **fuel cell** converts chemical energy into electricity. So does a battery, but a fuel cell is different because it can be refuelled, whereas a battery uses up its contents and has to be replaced or recharged. Fuel cells are also good because the only waste they produce is water.

HOW HYDROGEN FUEL CELLS WORK

If you burn hydrogen in oxygen you will get dihydrogen monoxide, a.k.a. water. If you do this reaction in a fuel cell it is possible to siphon off electrons from the hydrogen and pass them through a circuit to do work (e.g. lighting a bulb or driving a motor). Fuel cells can use pure hydrogen, which is difficult to store because it must be kept super-cold and tends to explode if there is a leak; or they can use other fuels like alcohol, which are converted into hydrogen.

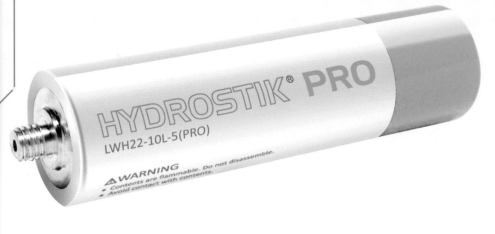

ABOVE...

THE HYDROSTIK IS A METAL HYDRIDE CARTRIDGE AVAILABLE TO BUY IN SHOPS.

FUEL CELLS TODAY

Fuel cells have several advantages: they convert lots of the energy from the chemicals into useful power; they supply a constant feed of electricity; and they come in different sizes from huge power plants for factories to tiny cartridges for laptops and mobile phones. A fuel cell about the size of a microwave oven can power a car.

Today a whole range of fuel cells are used by companies that have to make sure they never suffer power cuts (like Google); by the military when it needs to ship portable power plants to remote places; and by travellers who need long-lasting portable power sources.

FUTURE POWER

Fuel cells have a lot of problems. They are very expensive to build, and they need fuel, which has to come from somewhere. Hydrogen is hard to make and mostly comes from fossil fuels at the moment.

Researchers are working on these problems, and it is hoped that by 2025 fuel cells will be much cheaper, while hydrogen fuels could be widely produced using green power stations (see page 38). If the technology advances far enough, by 2025 fuel cells could routinely be powering cars, homes and businesses, and instead of stopping to fill up your car with petrol you could be refuelling at a hydrogen station.

ABOVE..
THE FUEL CELL "ENGINE" OF A VAUXHALL ZAFIRA.

ABOVE..............................
ELECTRIC CARS SUCH AS THIS BMW13 ARE ON THE ROAD NOW. CARS WITH FUEL CELL ENGINES ARE IN DEVELOPMENT.

RIGHT..............................
COULD ARTIFICIAL PLANTS HARVEST SUNLIGHT TO CREATE ELECTRICITY?

45

ARTIFICIAL PHOTOSYNTHESIS

Plants have a system of their own for converting one form of energy into another: **photosynthesis**. In photosynthesis, chemicals such as chlorophyll capture sunlight and use it to power an electrochemical reaction that turns water and carbon dioxide into sugar.

Researchers are racing to see if they can copy this process, and even improve on it (photosynthesis wastes a lot of sunlight). If they make this breakthrough, artificial plants could harvest sunlight to make both fuel and electricity directly.

THE FUTURE OF FLIGHT
PASSENGER PLANES AND AIRSHIPS

Air travel faces a number of problems over the next two decades. Planes burn huge quantities of expensive fuel, creating lots of pollution. Meanwhile, many passengers want to get where they are going faster. The aerospace industry has come up with some exciting answers to these challenges.

SWARMS AND SLINGSHOTS

Leading the pack is the aircraft manufacturer Airbus, which recently advanced some ambitious concepts.

To save fuel and make their planes more efficient, they have proposed that planes fly in swarms (i.e. close together), so that following planes experience less drag than the leader. This would require close control by advanced computer systems.

Planes use much of their fuel building up speed at take-off, so Airbus have suggested that a massive slingshot could be used to accelerate planes on the runway, catapulting them into the air at high speeds.

ABOVE..
AIRBUS'S CONCEPT FOR THE CABIN OF THE FUTURE.

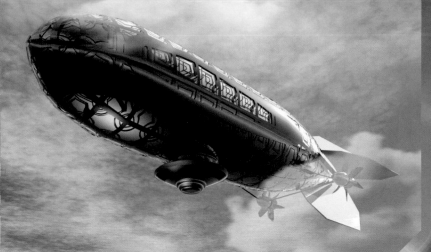

ABOVE...

THE VITALISING ZONE IS A VISION OF FUTURE
PASSENGER FLIGHT FROM AIRBUS.

FLYING WINGS

Other manufacturers have suggested new wing and body designs, such as wide, flat bodies that act like wings, generating their own lift (and known as flying wings or lifting bodies), or wrap-around wings to improve aerodynamics. NASA and Boeing have collaborated on the X-48 prototype, which uses the flying-wing shape to cut fuel use. Because of their shape, however, planes like this would have no passenger windows.

In contrast, Airbus have suggested that new materials might make it possible to have aircraft with transparent walls, so that passengers can have 360 views. Another development to improve passenger comfort could be morphing seats, which mould themselves to the individual.

LEFT...............................
THE AIRBUS CONCEPT
PLANE INCORPORATES
A PACKAGE OF NEW
TECHNOLOGIES

ONCE AND FUTURE AIRSHIPS

Before airplanes there were airships, also known as blimps, dirigibles or Zeppelins. These use bags of lighter-than-air gas, so that the aircraft does not need to spend energy getting and staying up in the air. Airships have had to overcome many technical problems: originally they used dangerously flammable hydrogen gas, and even today they have problems with ballast (heavy weights used to make the airship go up and down).

New airship designs claim to have overcome these problems, and the US military in particular has tried to develop airships for cargo lifting and surveillance. One solution is known as the Hybrid Air Vehicle — this is an airship where the balloon part is shaped like a large, fat wing, so that it generates its own lift like a plane wing, as well as from the helium inside it. According to its makers the HAV combines the best features of airships and airplanes, and is easier to control and land than a normal airship.

ABOVE..
THIS VISION OF A FUTURE AIRSHIP INCORPORATES
IMPROVED LIFT WITH GREEN TECHNOLOGY.

HIGH-FLYING VULTURE

Airship designs that are either in planning or already flying include the Long Endurance Multi-Intelligence Vehicle, which test flew in 2012, and the more ambitious Vulture programme. This involves a lightweight but gigantic wing, which stays permanently at high altitude as a cheap alternative to a satellite, and it may use airship technology as well as self-powering solar cells.

Airships could also be used to haul cargo, help traffic control and disaster-response teams with surveillance.

LEFT ....
AN ARTIST'S IMPRESSION OF THE KIND
OF AIRSHIP THAT WE COULD SEE IN
THE SKIES 15 YEARS FROM NOW.

FLYING CARS

Inventors have been dreaming of flying cars since before the first aeroplane, but it wasn't until the 1960s that the idea became popular. There was great optimism that new technology would revolutionize daily life for ordinary men and women, and the greatest symbol of this coming revolution was the idea of a car that could fly. Sixty years later this dream hasn't exactly come true, but in 2012 it finally became possible to buy a vehicle that you could both drive and fly.

ROADABLE AIRPLANES

The most successful early efforts to build a flying car were Robert Fulton's 1946 Airphibian and the related Aerocar designed and built by Moulton Taylor in the 1960s. Both were small road vehicles that could be turned into light aircraft by attaching tail and wing sections.

Driver-pilots still had the problem of finding a runaway for take-off and landing. In other words these vehicles were more like planes you could drive than cars you could fly, and in fact this type of vehicle is known as a "**roadable aircraft**". The latest and most advanced roadable aircraft is the Terrafugia Transition (right), which has folding wings and four wheels, but you still need a runway and a pilot's licence, not to mention $279,000 to buy one.

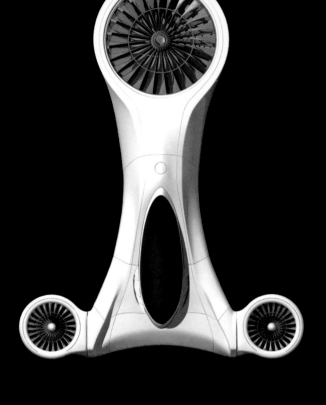

ABOVE...........................
THE AMAZING HAMMERHEAD FLIES USING THREE FANS THAT TILT AND THRUST.

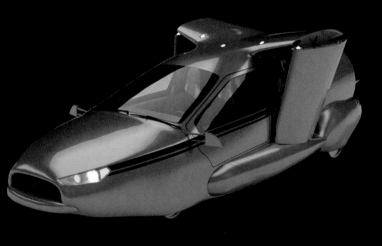

ABOVE AND LEFT...
THE TERRAFUGIA TRANSITION, A FLYING CAR THAT YOU CAN BUY TODAY.

SKYCARS AND FANCRAFT

A "real" flying car is one that can take off vertically from the middle of a traffic jam, fly across town and touch down outside your garage. The nearest thing to this today is the Moller Skycar, which combines the looks of a Ferrari with the power of four fan-blades. Also known as ducted propellors or shrouded rotors, these are like small helicopter rotors inside hoops or ducts. Because they are enclosed they are safer to use, produce lots of power, and can be angled for vertical take off and landing.

Other fan-bladed personal aerial vehicles (PAVs) in development include UrbanAero's X-Hawk and MACRO Industries SkyRider X2R.

ABOVE..
THE HAMMERHEAD TAKES OFF
AND LANDS VERTICALLY.

BELOW..
THE MOLLER SKYCAR AUTOMATES
FLIGHT CONTROLS, AND IS DESIGNED
FOR ANYONE WHO CAN DRIVE.

BELOW..
AUTOMATED SKYWAYS WILL MAKE IT SAFE FOR
HUGE NUMBERS OF VEHICLES TO FLY AT ONCE.

SKYWAYS

Flying cars could cause real problems – millions of small aircraft buzzing around could lead to carnage in the skies. Advances in computer control and navigation, however, should create "skyways" – highways in the sky. In fact NASA is co-ordinating a "highway-in-the-sky" project, which aims to integrate GPS and automated-sensor technology with augmented-reality screens to generate computer-drawn skyways for driver-pilots to follow, while computers prevent collisions.

A NEW AGE OF SAIL
KITESHIPS AND FLOATING CITIES

Hundreds of years ago, ships used wind power to get around. Ships with sails gave way to ones with engines, but the advantages that wind offers are still the same today as in the great age of sail. The wind is free to use, weighs nothing, causes no pollution and never runs out.

The same cannot be said for bunker fuel, the type of oil that most ships run on. Bunker fuel is the dirtiest and most polluting form of vehicle fuel, and carbon dioxide emissions from shipping are growing all the time.

SKYSAILS

To solve these problems some shipping companies are exploring the idea of using new spins on sailing technology to harness the power of the wind, cut their fuel bills and reduce pollution.

One idea is the **kiteship**, a normal cargo vessel fitted with a giant kite or skysail that can be automatically winched back in and folded away when the wind is not blowing. By flying the skysail at a relatively high altitude, the ship can take advantage of high wind speeds. Many racing yachts already have special sails called kites, which can be fitted to the tip of the mast to extract the last ounce of power from the wind, and the kiteship is a scaled up version of this.

VERTICAL WINGS

Another idea is to replace the fabric sails of a normal sailing ship with metal wings, similar to those on a plane but vertical.

Researchers at the University of Tokyo have designed the Wind Challenger Project, a system of retractable metal wings or aerofoils. These rise from the deck and are rotated until edge on to the wind. Just as an airplane's wings generate lift, a force pushing the wings up, so the aerofoil sails generate a force pushing the wings, and the attached boat. The computer-controlled sails can be rotated, and in stormy weather they can telescope down into the hull.

Sails of similar appearance are a feature of B9 Shipping's planned cargo ship, which uses the Dyna-rig system of rigid sails that have no rigging and sit on rotating masts. This design also makes use of a skysail, and will fuel its engine with eco-friendly biogas made by recycling waste food.

LEFT..
THE STATE-OF-THE-ART B9 SAILSHIP COULD BE
CREATED FROM EXISTING TECHNOLOGY.

BELOW...
LILYPAD ECOPOLIS IS A VISION OF A FUTURE HOME
FOR "CLIMATE REFUGEES" DISPLACED BY THE EFFECTS
OF GLOBAL WARMING OVER THE NEXT CENTURY.

FLOATING CITIES AND SEAGOING SKYSCRAPERS

New sailing ships are not the only bold idea planned for the
oceans. A variety of exciting new projects imagine whole
communities at sea, on artificial islands, floating cities
or giant ocean-going marine observatories. For instance,
the Sea Orbiter project, supposedly set to launch in 2014,
is a skyscraper-like ocean laboratory, observatory and
exploration vessel that will extend over 30 m down below
the surface as well as over 20 m above the surface.

RIGHT...
THE SEA ORBITER IS LIKE A POINTED ICEBERG,
WITH MOST OF ITS MASS BELOW WATER LEVEL.

53

BEAM ME UP
LASER-POWERED LIGHTCRAFT

A revolutionary technology straight out of science fiction would see saucer-shaped spaceships known as **lightcraft** accelerated to hypersonic speeds by blasting them with lasers fired from space. It would be possible to travel anywhere in the world within 45 minutes, or out into space at a fraction of the cost of today's rockets.

With orbiting power plants, rotating spacecraft, super-conducting electromagnetic propulsion and ion thrusters, this incredible scheme pushes the boundaries of the scientific imagination but is entirely based on existing technology.

The most expensive part of getting into space is the amount of fuel required to blast a rocket free of Earth's gravity. At launch, the recently defunct Space Shuttle with its booster rockets was over 90% fuel by weight. But what if a spaceship didn't need to carry any fuel? This is the logic behind the lightcraft concept.

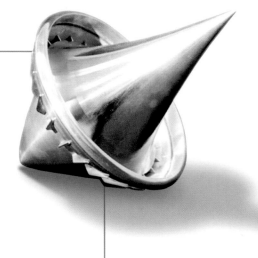

RIGHT..............................
A METAL "SPINNING TOP" USED IN TESTING THE PHYSICS OF LIGHTCRAFT.

FAR RIGHT......................
RESEARCHERS TESTING A "SPINNING TOP".

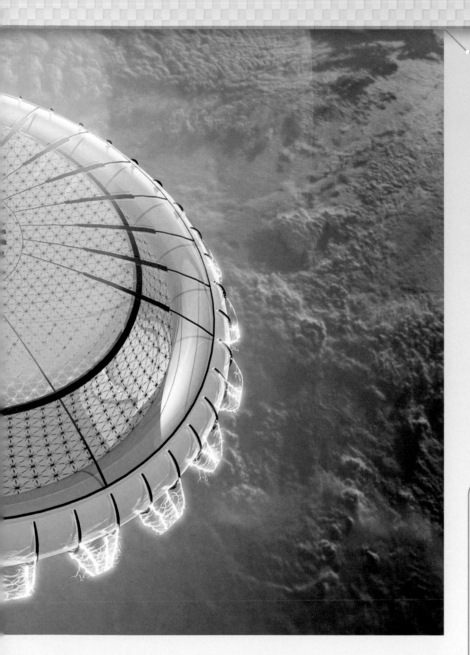

BEAM PROPULSION

The bottom or sides of a lightcraft are dish-shaped mirrors. When a laser or similarly intense beam of energy hits the mirror, it is focused onto a point directly behind the craft, heating the air to a temperature hotter than the surface of the Sun. The intense heat instantly vaporizes the air, creating an explosive shockwave that blasts the lightcraft forward. Every pulse of laser light that hits the craft creates another explosion, and the spring of explosions accelerates it to great speed. This is called beam propulsion.

This is the basic concept of a lightcraft. At the moment experiments have been limited to small polished metal objects that look like toy spinning tops, but there are at least two plans for full-size lightcraft. One plan, developed by beam-propulsion pioneer Dr Leik Myrabo and the Umea Institute, calls for a scaled-up version of the spinning-top design.

ABOVE.........................
THE MICROWAVE LIGHTCRAFT CONCEPT FROM NASA.

BELOW.........................
CONCEPT FOR A LIGHTSHIP AND LAUNCH PLATFORM, FROM AURORA SPACELINES.

FLYING SAUCERS

An even more ambitious design, co-developed by Myrabo with NASA, uses **masers** – microwave lasers – fired from an orbiting satellite. The satellite collects sunlight to power the microwave beam and fires it down onto a saucer-shaped lightcraft, which has collecting mirrors that can route the power to one side of the craft, causing a string of explosions that accelerate it sideways. Once it is going fast enough the lightcraft turns so that it is lying flat, face-on to the airstream.

The lightcraft now focuses the maser beam ahead of it to create an airspike – a bubble of superheated air that explodes in front of the lightcraft. Immediately behind the airspike's explosive shockwave there is no air, just a vacuum, which means the lightcraft experiences no air resistance or drag, and can accelerate to about 30,000 km/h using electromagnetically powered **ion drives** around its edge.

To get off the ground in the first place, the main body of the lightcraft is circled by a helium-filled hoop, so that it can take off like an airship (see page 47).

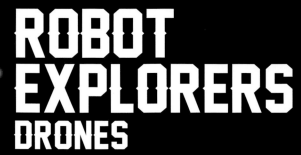

ROBOT EXPLORERS
DRONES

"Drone" is a general term for a remote-control vehicle or robot of some sort. Today it usually means an **unmanned air vehicle** (UAV), a radio-controlled small aircraft such as the Predator drones used by the US military, but drones can come in all shapes and sizes, and can be found on land, sea and air.

For instance, the robot submarines known as ROVs (remotely operated vehicles — see page 77) are a type of drone, as are bomb disposal robots used by the police and military. A drone is a sort of telepresence robot (see page 8).

THE CHEAP ALTERNATIVE

Drones are already familiar from military use, but over the next 15 years they are likely to become common everywhere. The coming drone explosion will change society.

People are both valuable and expensive, and getting them to travel somewhere is even more expensive. Why send a reporter and camera crew to a remote war-torn district when you can send a drone for a fraction of the price and with no risk of it being kidnapped?

Drones can perform hundreds of useful jobs, from cleaning the ocean to gathering news. They can also do more sinister tasks; it is feared that in the near future the skies over our cities may become filled with camera-equipped drones watching and recording us, as part of a growing **surveillance state**.

TOP AND ABOVE ....
THE RQ-4A GLOBAL HAWK IS A RECONNAISSANCE DRONE USED BY THE US MILITARY.

KEEPING AN EYE OUT

Some of these hopes and fears are science fiction at the moment. The drones in use today are mostly essentially expensive radio-controlled aircraft, such as the quadcopter drones (lightweight flying robots with four mini-rotors) used for news-gathering in Nebraska, USA, but there is a huge range of experimental drones already at prototype stage.

For instance, the Electric Power Research Institute is developing small UAV drones to fly out after a storm and locate downed power lines, while the US coastguard is considering ordering Piranha unmanned boat drones.

LEFT..
SATOORN IS A FRENCH-DESIGNED UAV
THAT CAN BE USED INSIDE BUILDINGS.

MICRO-UAVS

Already taking flight in the laboratory are several micro-UAVS — tiny remote-controlled aircraft. Quadcopters are widely available as toys, and programs have been developed to make them fly as swarms. Dragonflies, bees and birds have inspired biomimetic micro-UAVs. For instance, the SilMach dragonfly drone uses flapping wings to propel itself.

Bounce Imaging have developed the Smart Ball, a small sphere packed with sensors that can be tossed into damaged buildings or dropped down dangerous holes to send back information to rescuers.

ABOVE..............................
SILMACH'S DRAGONFLY
SURVEILLANCE MICRODRONE
IS ONLY 6 CM WIDE.

LEFT................................
THE NANO HUMMINGBIRD
FROM AEROVIRONMENT IS
ONLY SLIGHTLY LARGER
THAN THAN A REAL BIRD.

CLEANING THE OCEANS

Drones don't have to stick to just looking. Suggestions for useful drone activities include fleets of small drones similar to existing Roomba vacuum-cleaning robots, which can be scattered into the sea to clean up oil spills, and plastic-eating drone submarines that could wander the ocean picking up the plastic rubbish that has been dumped by humans.

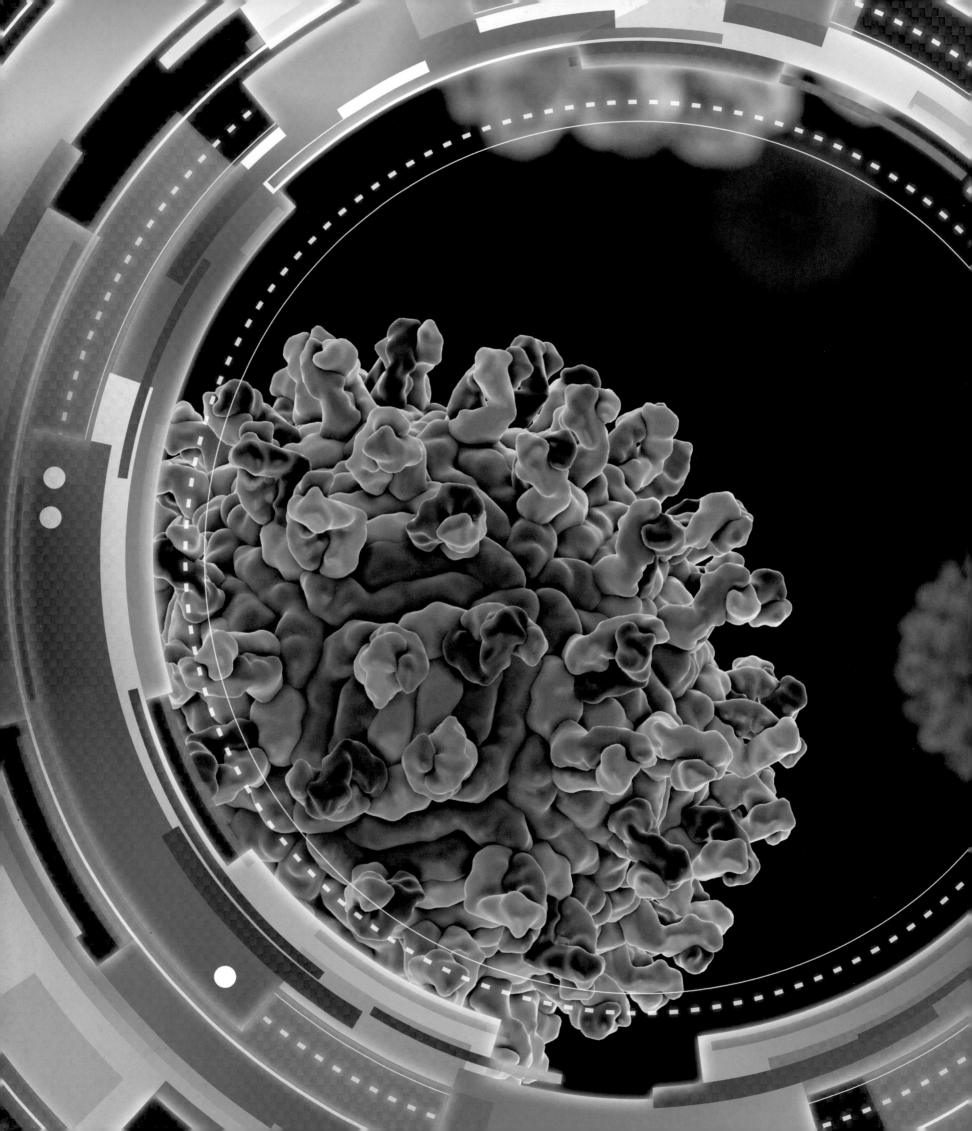

MEDICINE AND BIOTECHNOLOGY

Medicine is still waiting for the super apps of the genetic engineering revolution, but they could be on their way, and they will have a huge impact on all aspects of life, not just health and medicine.

Treatments and even cures for important and deadly diseases could be on the way thanks to genetic biotech. Robotics big and small could also make an impact on health, from tiny nanobots that patrol your blood vessels to bionic arms and legs for the disabled.

Biotech may even make it possible to bring extinct species back to life.

HEART-HEALING MINI-MACHINES
MEDICAL NANOBOTS

In the 1966 science fiction movie *Fantastic Voyage*, a submarine is shrunk to microscopic size and injected into the bloodstream of an injured man, on a mission to save his life by swimming through his blood vessels and performing laser surgery from within.

Today the world's leading research institutes are working on making this into science fact, by creating nanomachines little bigger than atoms, which might soon be able to patrol our bodies.

SMALLEST OF THE SMALL

"Nano" means "tiny", and nanomachines are machines built on the nanometre scale. To give you an idea of how small that is, find a ruler and look at the smallest intervals, which show millimetres. Now imagine splitting that into a million smaller intervals — these would show nanometres. A human hair is typically around 90,000 nanometres across. Nanomachines are built from individual molecules or even just a few atoms.

A NEW INDUSTRIAL REVOLUTION

Think about the impact the Industrial Revolution had on the world. Big machines were able to take over many complicated tasks. But most of them are too big for jobs at the level of molecules.

Nanomachines could change all that, doing the same kinds of jobs as big machines but with individual atoms and molecules. For instance, **nanobots** are nanoscale robots: tiny machines that can move about, pick things up and even destroy things. They could make it possible to inject tiny robots into the bloodstream to attack germs, clear blocked arteries and fix broken nerve or muscle cells.

60

ABOVE...
AN ARTIST'S IMPRESSION OF A MEDICAL NANOBOT AT WORK ON A BLOOD CELL.

BUBBLE-POWERED NANOROCKETS

Scientists have already created bubble-powered rocket nanobots in the laboratory. A layer of material a few atoms thick is rolled into a tube and filled with hydrogen peroxide, which reacts with water to make bubbles. When placed into water, the tiny rocket shoots a stream of bubbles out of one end, driving it forwards.

Another design uses a tube coated with zinc. When dropped into acid (such as in the human stomach), the zinc reacts to create bubbles of hydrogen gas, blasting the rocket at speeds of up to 100 times its own length per second. If the nanorocket were fitted with molecules that can recognize and destroy germs, it could be let loose inside your body to help protect you.

Other nanoparticles have already been developed to carry luminous blobs of chemical. The other end of the nanoparticle is fitted with a molecule that sticks onto diseased cells. When a dose of these nanoparticles is injected into the body, they find their target and light up, so that doctors can locate the problem when they scan the patient.

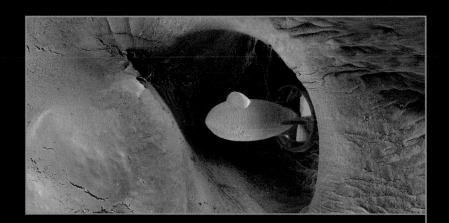

FUTURE NANOBOTS

In the future, nanobots could be built that can live inside the body for long periods, find their own way around and locate trouble spots. Some could be equipped as hunter-killers to track down viruses, bacteria and cancerous cells. Others could be fitted with cutting equipment to clear away plaques, the fatty build-ups that clog arteries.

ABOVE RIGHT..
A NANOSUBMARINE, CREATED BY MICROTEC, TRAVELS THROUGH AN ARTERY.

61

BIONIC PEOPLE
PROSTHETICS AND ENHANCEMENTS

The stars of the 2012 Paralympic Games were the Blade Runners – lower leg amputees whose missing limbs were replaced with springy blade-like prosthetics (a prosthetic is an artificial body part). These hi-tech blades made from advanced materials are so good at storing and releasing energy that they have caused a big argument over whether they do not simply make up for disability, but might even boost human performance.

Exciting new technology like blades is transforming the world of prosthetics. Recent advances mean that prosthetic feet, hands and other parts that function as well as the real thing will soon be available, and by 2025 artificial limbs could be better than the real thing.

TYPES OF PROSTHESIS

Prosthetic legs come in three categories: ordinary prostheses, which are basically similar to the wooden legs of old; energy storing-and-returning (ESR) feet, which use springs and small motors to mimic the action of natural feet, ankles and legs; and **bionic** legs, which are connected to the user's nervous system making it possible to control them directly.

62

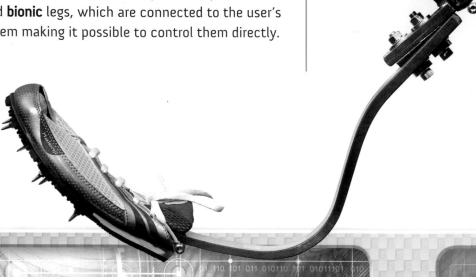

ABOVE
BRITISH ATHLETE JONNIE PEACOCK WINS THE 100 M SPRINT AT THE 2012 PARALYMPICS.

LEFT
PROSTHETIC LEGS NOW USE SPRINGS TO MIMIC NATURAL MOTION.

TENTACLE ARMS AND FINGER TOOLS

By 2025 bionic hands and feet won't just give disabled users normal function; they will actually be able to give them extra abilities, maybe even super powers: extra strength and endurance, infinitely rotating wrists and bendable fingers; extra fingers with changeable tools. A radical concept that is already available in crude form is a prosthetic tentacle; in the future an amputee might choose to have something like an elephant's trunk fitted instead of an arm.

FEET 2.0

The Belgian Ankle Mimicking Prosthetic Foot (AMP foot) prosthesis is a recent breakthrough in ESR technology. Natural feet have tendons that store the energy of the stride as the foot lands and the ankle bends, releasing it to help lift the foot back up. Many ESR feet already include such springs. But natural feet also have leg muscles to add power to the foot/ankle action, and the AMP foot includes a lightweight motor that mimics natural muscles. Another team from America has adapted rocket-fuel technology for a super-lightweight motor in their ESR design — the motor uses solid propellant similar to that used in some rockets.

Meanwhile, the Rehabilitation Institute of Chicago recently developed a bionic leg that can respond to the user's nervous system. The RIC Bionic leg works so well that amputee Zac Vawter used one to complete the world's tallest indoor stair climb event, SkyRise, climbing the 103 floors of the Willis Tower in Chicago. A company called bebionic has developed a bionic hand that responds to signals from nerves in the upper arm of the user, making it possible to open bottles, make a fist and even type, with the fingers controlled by thought alone.

INVISIBLE MUSCLE SUITS

Eventually bionics might advance to the point where a completely paralysed person could bionically control a wearable exoskeleton (see page 13).

Made up of thin, lightweight struts and artificial muscle meshes that can be tailored like clothes, a "muscle suit" could be worn like a wetsuit, hidden under clothes.

HACKING NATURE
BIOENGINEERING AND CLONING

What if we could solve the global food crisis by growing meat in a test tube? What if we could cure illness by spraying a cloud of special viruses down our throats? And what if we could bring extinct creatures back to life, so that you could see a real, live mammoth at the zoo?

BELOW.............................
AN ARTIST'S IMPRESSION OF A HERD OF MAMMOTHS. COULD WE SOON SEE THIS FOR REAL?

THE VACANTI MOUSE

Thanks to bioengineering, all these fantasies might come true. Bioengineering means changing the way nature works through the use of technology. One example is the growth of animal cells in the laboratory. In a famous experiment in 1997, a US scientist implanted a laboratory-grown ear (made from cow cells) into the back of a mouse, proving that it is possible to grow replacement body parts.

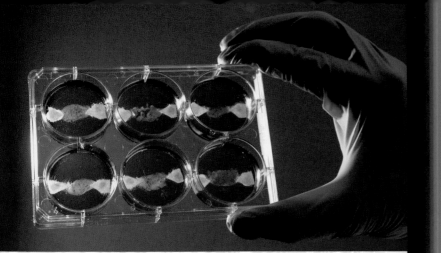

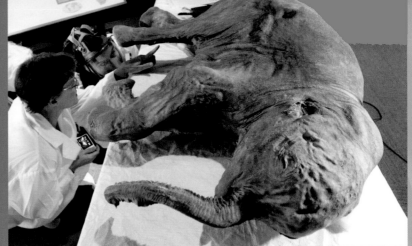

TEST-TUBE MEAT

More recent research has enabled the growth of replacement parts for human kidneys, but in the future it might be possible to grow new parts for the eye, the heart, the spinal cord, the liver and the bones and muscles.

Human cells are not the only ones that can be bioengineered. Scientists are working on ways to grow animal muscle cells in the lab. If they succeed, in a decade's time you could be eating a beefburger made from meat that has never been anywhere near a cow.

ABOVE..
ANIMAL CELLS BEING GROWN IN A PETRI DISH.

GENETIC ENGINEERING

Genetic engineering occurs when scientists tinker with the genetic makeup of a living organism. Every organism has a genetic code made from **DNA**, which is carried inside every cell. This blueprint contains the instructions for making and running the organism, and these instructions can be changed.

For example, some genetic diseases could be cured by use of a virus that can inject its own genes into your DNA. Genetic engineers insert a healthy version of the malfunctioning gene into the virus, infect the patient with the virus and let the virus inject the healthy gene into every cell in the patient.

The first gene therapy to become commercially available in the West uses an engineered virus called Glybera to treat a rare disorder called lipoprotein lipase deficiency. Gene therapies are also under development for conditions from haemophilia to Parkinson's, so by 2025 it may be routine to treat disease by spraying an engineered virus down your throat so it can get into your bloodstream.

THE REAL JURASSIC PARK

Cloning is growing an identical copy of an animal by implanting its DNA into an egg, which then develops into an adult animal. Scientists in Brazil recently announced plans to clone several species that are in danger of becoming extinct. In the film *Jurassic Park*, scientists use dinosaur DNA to clone dinosaurs, but the dinosaurs died out 65 million years ago and DNA cannot survive this long.

However, DNA has been recovered from the bodies of frozen mammoths. It could well be possible to clone these and other extinct animals. For instance, DNA could be taken from a mammoth corpse and inserted into the egg of an elephant, which would grow into a baby mammoth carried by a female elephant.

Other extinct animals that could be brought back from the dead include the sabre-toothed cat, the dodo, the giant sloth, the moa and the thylacine wolf.

ABOVE...
SCIENTISTS COULD RECOVER
DNA FROM FROZEN MAMMOTHS
LIKE THIS ONE.

RIGHT..............................
MODEL DNA STRANDS.

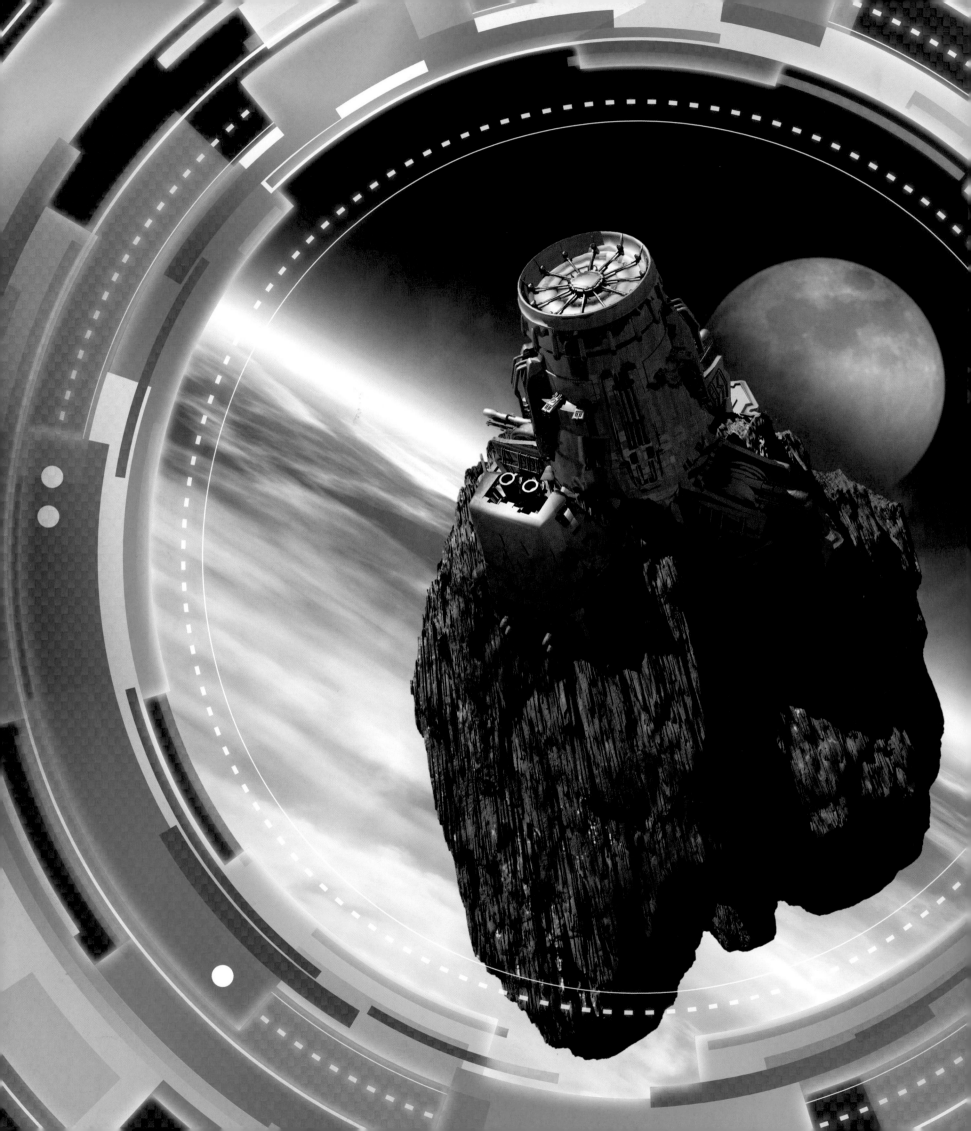

EXPLORATION

Exciting developments in space travel mean that within 20 years many people will be able to afford a trip into space. Private space travel is driving the space industry forward at its fastest rate in decades, with private spacecraft already delivering supplies to the International Space Station.

Advanced technology is being aimed down as well as up, with hi-tech submarines exploring the extremes of the ocean and undersea mining colonies harvesting the riches of the deep.

TICKET TO THE MOON
PRIVATE SPACE FLIGHT

Rockets developed, built and flown by governments tend to be expensive. The biggest rocket available to the US government, the Delta 4, costs around $435 million per launch.

Space Shuttle launches were similarly expensive, so when the Space Shuttle fleet was coming to the end of its lifespan NASA decided to use private companies to send supplies to the International Space Station (ISS).

PRIVATE COMPANIES

The Commercial Orbital Transportation Services project was started in 2006, opening up a new world of private space travel, in which rockets are developed, built and flown by private companies, and NASA is just a customer.

As a result, costs for getting into space are coming down fast. SpaceX, the leading private space company, is developing a rocket called Falcon Heavy that can carry twice as much as Delta 4 for $100 million per launch, so that the cost per ton is $1.8 million: 1/10th as much as the government rocket!

DRAGONS AND GRASSHOPPERS

In 2012 SpaceX successfully made the first commercial resupply of the International Space Station (ISS) with its Dragon capsule, launched by Falcon 9 rockets. The Dragon capsule is reusable: after delivering its load of supplies it is filled up with equipment to bring back to Earth, and then splashes down in the ocean.

SpaceX is contracted to do 11 more supply missions to the ISS, and also intends to develop the Dragon capsule as a crewed module so it can be used to carry people into orbit and maybe beyond. SpaceX is also developing the Grasshopper rocket, a vertical takeoff and landing rocket stage that will make launch rockets reusable, so that they become even cheaper. As the cost of getting into orbit tumbles, it will be possible for everyone from private companies to universities and even schools to send satellites and experiments into orbit.

ABOVE...
SPACEX STAFF SHOW HOW THE DRAGON
COULD BE ADAPTED TO CARRY CREW.

LEFT...
THE SPACEX DRAGON TAKING CARGO
TO THE INTERNATIONAL SPACE STATION.

MOON EXPRESS

SpaceX is just one of several projects now in development, which aim to make private space travel a reality.

Moon Express wants to set up what it calls a "lunar railroad", a programme of missions to the Moon that will start with robotic landers and probes. These will explore the Moon, looking for ice and precious minerals, and later a permanent human colony will be set up on the Moon.

A moon base could be a vital stepping stone for missions to Mars. Alternatively, Martian missions could start off from space stations orbiting the Earth. Bigelow Aerospace is planning to sell cheap inflatable space stations to companies developing these plans.

BELOW..
INFLATABLE SPACE STATIONS COULD BE USED TO
CREATE A BASE ON THE MOON.

ORBITAL AIRSHIPS AND SPACE ELEVATORS

Other private companies are exploring revolutionary ways of getting into space that don't use rockets. JP Aerospace's Airship to Orbit plan involves using airships to lift heavy loads high into the atmosphere without needing expensive fuel. V-shaped flying wing airships, over a mile long, then accelerate the loads into orbit.

Even more ambitious is the **space elevator** project, which would run a thin but extremely strong wire from an orbiting space station down to the surface of the Earth. The wire would be used as an elevator cable, allowing capsules to run up and down and providing a permanent bridge into space.

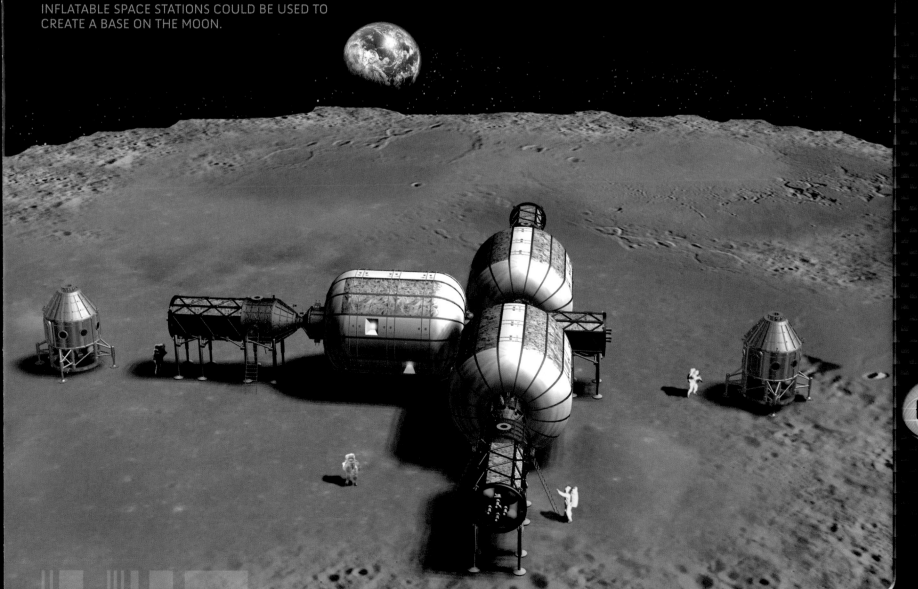

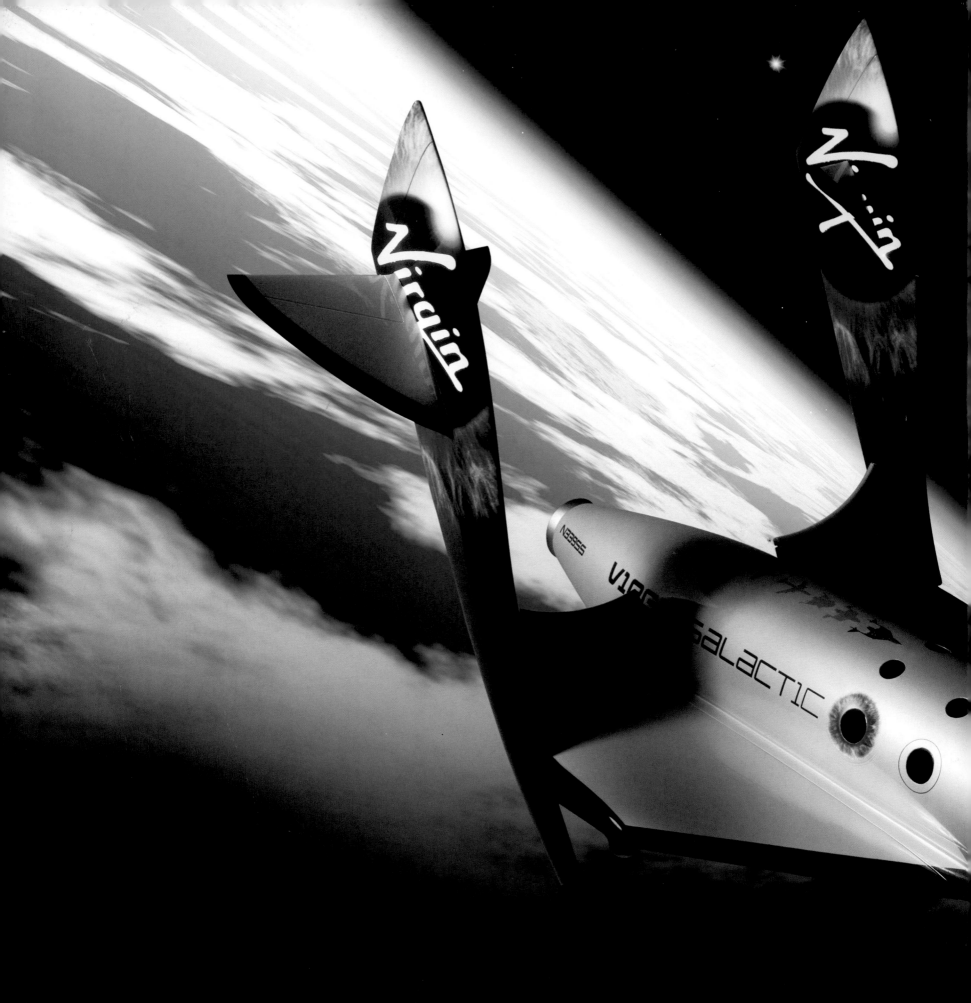

SPACE TOURISM

Space is about to become a top holiday destination. There are at least six private companies battling to be the first to get tourists into outer space, using both tried-and-tested rocket technology and cutting-edge new rocketplanes and mini-shuttles. Alongside these "spacelines", there are plans for space hotels, spaceports and even travel insurance for astro-tourists.

The dream is that in the near future flights into space will become routine and relatively cheap, with thousands of people experiencing the thrills of weightlessness and the joy of seeing the Earth from space.

VISIT SPACE

Virgin Galactic's SpaceShipTwo is likely to be the first vessel to actually carry space tourists. Here's how the journey will work.

1 ___At an altitude of 15.5 km (50,000 ft), SpaceShipTwo launches from the mothership.

2 ___At 100 km (328,00 ft), SpaceShipTwo reaches the Kármán line, where passengers become astronauts.

3 ___110 km (361,000 ft) is Virgin Galactic's maximum planned altitude. SpaceShipTwo raises its wings after the rockets ignite.

4 __Re-entry into the atmosphere in the wing-raised ("feathered") position.

5 __At 21.5 km (70,000 ft) SpaceShipTwo defeathers into glider mode.

6 __SpaceShipTwo glides home.

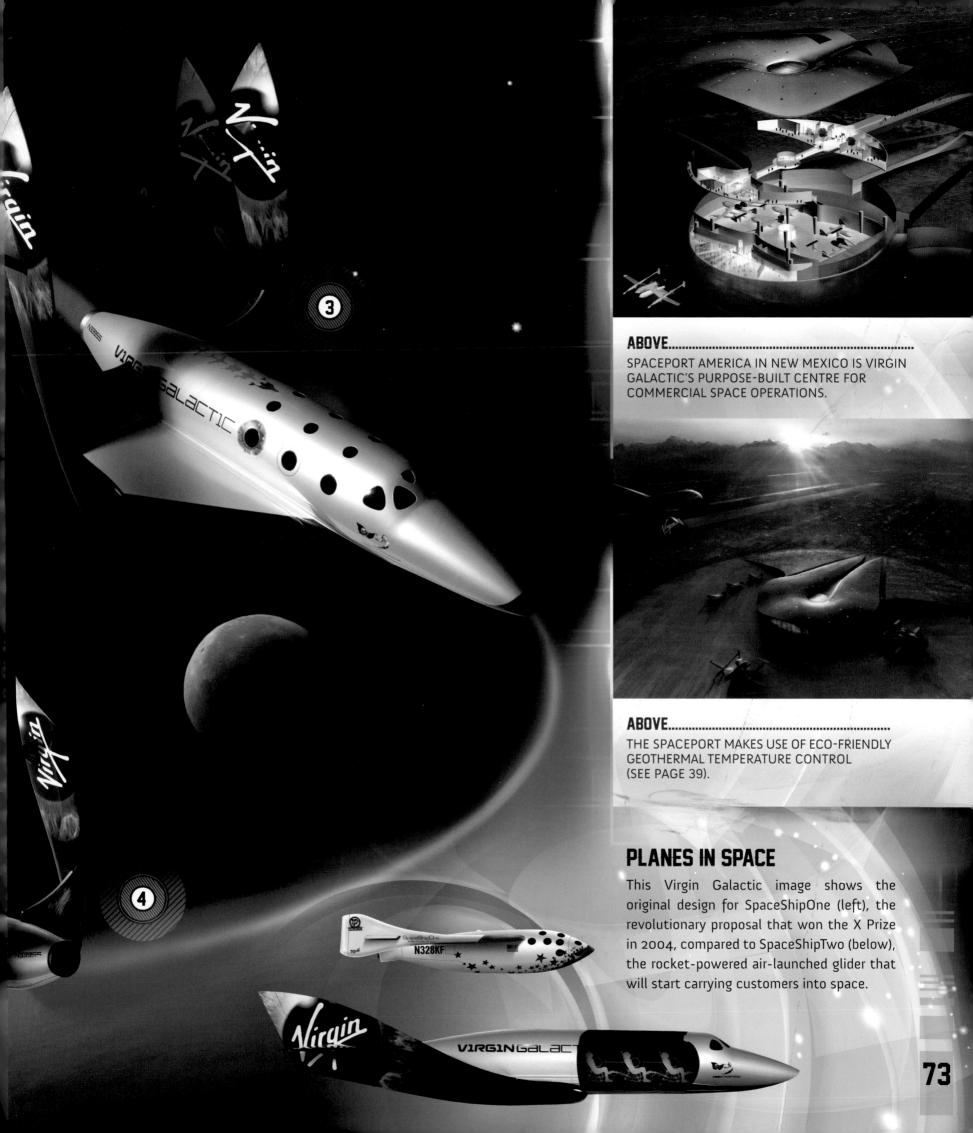

③

④

ABOVE..
SPACEPORT AMERICA IN NEW MEXICO IS VIRGIN
GALACTIC'S PURPOSE-BUILT CENTRE FOR
COMMERCIAL SPACE OPERATIONS.

ABOVE..
THE SPACEPORT MAKES USE OF ECO-FRIENDLY
GEOTHERMAL TEMPERATURE CONTROL
(SEE PAGE 39).

PLANES IN SPACE

This Virgin Galactic image shows the
original design for SpaceShipOne (left), the
revolutionary proposal that won the X Prize
in 2004, compared to SpaceShipTwo (below),
the rocket-powered air-launched glider that
will start carrying customers into space.

TREASURE FROM OUTER SPACE
ASTEROID MINING

Earth is short of resources. Yet our planet is floating in a sea of valuable minerals – huge chunks of them, waiting for the prospectors of the future to launch a new gold rush... in outer space!

These minerals are contained in asteroids, rocks left over from the formation of the Solar System that hurtle around between the planets. A single 500 m wide asteroid could be loaded with up to $3 trillion of platinum, or enough water to fuel and supply rocket missions that would cost in excess of $5 trillion to launch from Earth.

These staggering sums of money have inspired a group of adventurous millionaires to fund an ambitious new project called Planetary Resources, which is pioneering the concept of **asteroid mining**. Although their plan sounds like science fiction, it is based on solid fact.

NEAR-EARTH OBJECTS

Most asteroids in the Solar System are based in the Asteroid Belt between Mars and Jupiter. But for mining to be affordable, it is necessary to look to asteroids nearer to home: so-called near-Earth objects (NEOs).

The good news is that a 2011 sky survey by NASA's WISE space telescope revealed that there are probably twice as many NEOs within relatively easy reach of Earth as previously thought. Planetary Resources estimate that there are 1500 NEOs that would be easier to reach than the Moon.

LEFT..
A COMPUTER SIMULATION OF ASTEROID MINING.

BELOW........................
THE FUEL HARVESTER CONCEPT
BY DEEP SPACE INDUSTRIES.

RIGHT........................
AN ARKYD 100 LEO SATELLITE,
TO BE USED IN STUDYING NEOS.

BELOW........................
THE FUEL HARVESTER
PROCESSING PLANT.

ASTEROID HUNTERS

The Planetary Resources plan is to launch a series of Arkyd 100 Leo satellites to hunt for suitable asteroids. The Leo space telescopes are revolutionary in terms of their low cost. Combined with the rapidly falling cost of getting into orbit (see page 68), the Leo design will make it economically possible for a private company to put a fleet of space telescopes into orbit.

By adding abilities, such as ion drives (cheap rocket engines that use electromagnets to speed up charged particles of gas and fire them backwards, propelling the spaceship forwards) and extra sensors to Leo satellites, Planetary Resources will create Interceptor and Rendezvous Prospector satellites. These will travel to target asteroids and scan them to check whether they are suitable for mining.

FACTORIES IN SPACE

The technology to mine asteroids has yet to be invented, but research is underway.

Swarms of small robots will dig trenches on the surface of an asteroid, sucking up chunks of rock and crushing them into powder. The ore will then have to be melted and refined to produce minerals; this could involve gigantic space-going factories. Asteroids made mostly of water ice could be swallowed whole by "envelope" spacecraft.

These operations will be easier if carried out close to home, so resource-rich asteroids will probably be captured and brought back to near Earth space. Asteroids could be fitted with ion drives or "pushed" by firing lasers at them.

SUNKEN GOLD
MINING THE DEEP OCEAN BOTTOM

In 2012 film-maker and adventurer James Cameron became only the third person, and the first since 1960, to visit the deepest part of the ocean: the Challenger Deep at the bottom of the Marianas Trench in the Pacific.

Cameron had funded the development of the Deepsea Challenger, a vertical torpedo-style sub with tall banks of super-bright LED lights on top of a tiny bubble of steel where the pilot sits. It's one of a new breed of underwater vehicles promising to open up the biggest yet most mysterious part of our planet. It beat competition from three other deep ocean submersibles, including Virgin Oceanic's DeepFlight Challenger, and Deepsearch, a sub partly funded by one of the founders of Google.

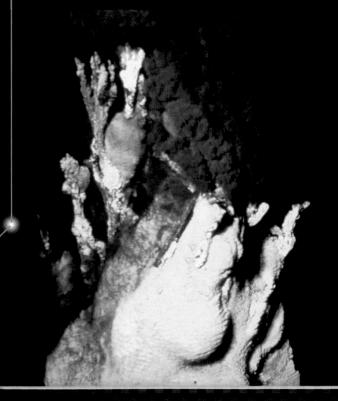

HOT SPOTS

The goal of these projects, apart from setting records, is to explore an undiscovered realm. We know more about the surface of the Moon than we do about the bottom of the oceans, yet 71% of the surface of our planet is seafloor.

Some of the potentially most valuable locations are where volcanic activity causes mineral-laden mud and superheated water to blast out of cracks in the ocean floor. Known as hydrothermal vents or black smokers, they feature water hotter than 100°, crushing pressure and poisonous chemicals, yet teem with life.

LEFT..
A BLACK SMOKER ON THE FLOOR OF THE PACIFIC.

ABOVE..
THE DEEPSEA CHALLENGER HAS A VIEWPORT FOR THE PILOT NEAR ITS BASE.

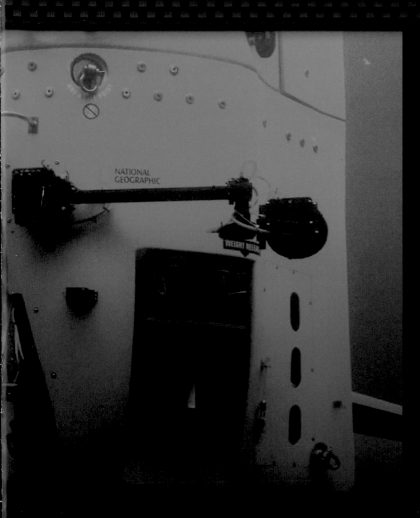

BOTTOM FEEDERS

Mining the ocean floor deposits will require trenching and cutting machines (robots equipped with mechanical diggers and rock-crushing teeth), which will "eat" chimneys and carve rock from the bottom, chewing it up into powdered rock. Suction devices could vacuum up the crushed rock, pumping it to barges on the surface for processing.

The Chinese are working on a nuclear-powered deep-sea mining station and mothership system that could work in the open ocean around for the clock for months at a time.

BELOW..
ROBOTIC HARVESTING OF MINERAL
DEPOSITS FROM THE SEA BED.

PROSPECTING THE OCEAN FLOOR

Of great interest to mineral prospectors are the chimneys or columns of mineral-rich rock that form around hydrothermal vents. If these could be "harvested", trillions of dollars of valuable minerals, including gold, would be available.

Several companies are working on deep ocean mining. Nautilus Minerals, for instance, is preparing to send teams of remotely operated submarines to identify the richest pickings.

ROV (remotely operated vehicle) technology has advanced greatly, with mini-submarines that either swim free or are tethered to a mothership on the surface. Using powerful lights, stereo cameras and other sensors, ROVs will identify the richest fields of minerals before teams of heavy-duty mining robots are sent down.

POISONOUS HARVEST

Deep sea mining could help to prevent important mineral resources from running out, but would almost certainly cause great environmental damage. Hydrothermal vents are fragile and important ecosystems, so it seems ethically questionable to grind them into powder. Deep sea mining would probably also kick up clouds of toxic chemicals, while the barges at the surface would release floods of polluted water.

BUILDING THE FUTURE
INVENTING 21ˢᵀ-CENTURYSTYLE

Inventors are not just lone geniuses who work in a cluttered lab, shouting "Eureka!" when lightbulbs appear above their heads. Most inventors work as part of large organisations like Apple or Google.

For independent inventors and those who work for companies and universities, the way that inventing is done is going to change over the next 15 years. The changes may be merely huge, or they may be even bigger!

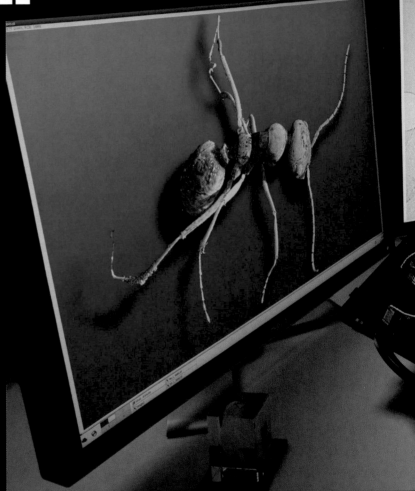

VIRTUAL DESIGN

Computers have already changed the way inventing is done. Inventors can now design and engineer their inventions in cyberspace rather than the real world, and this trend will continue.

Using virtual reality goggles and gloves, for instance, inventors will get inside magnified virtual models of their designs, moving pieces around with their hands and studying their inventions at work from the inside.

RAPID PROTOTYPING

After design, the next stage of inventing is making a prototype, where you create a physical model of your invention. This used to be expensive and time-consuming, but 3D printers have revolutionized this stage of inventing by offering what is called "rapid prototyping".

It's now possible to print out numerous different versions of your model, and if they don't work, it's no big deal – simply put them in the recycling, tweak the design and try again.

Rapid prototyping will speed up the process of turning ideas into reality.

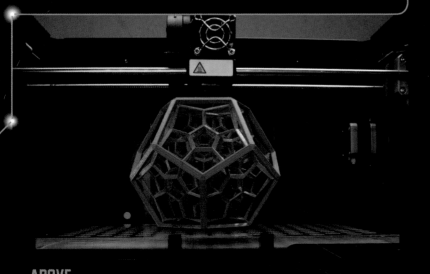

ABOVE ....
3D PRINTERS LIKE THE MAKERBOT REPLICATOR ARE A HUGE HELP TO INDEPENDENT INVENTORS.

COMPUTER-ASSISTED INVENTING

But what about the crucial first phase of inventing – coming up with an idea in the first place?

This is where the greatest revolution could be about to happen. Artificial intelligence (AI) researchers are trying to build computers that can come up with original thoughts (see page 10), especially original ideas for inventions.

One approach that is already being tried is called the evolutionary algorithm, which mimics the way evolution works in nature. It's a computer program that comes up with lots of different ideas and then tests them to see which ones are worth keeping. It rejects bad ideas and uses good ones as the basis for slightly different new ideas.

The algorithm has to go through millions of repeats before it comes up with a decent idea, but because it's running on a computer, this doesn't take long. Genetic algorithms are already helping to come up with new inventions.

If AI ever achieves real intelligence, the smart machines that would result could start coming up with new inventions much faster than humans can manage. This could bring about the greatest change in human history, known as the Singularity. If this ever happens – and some people predict it could happen before 2025 – it won't just be inventing that changes forever.

CROWDFUNDING

Inventions can't change the world if they never make it out of the lab, so the next step is turning a prototype into a product. In the past this stage was probably the hardest for independent inventors, since only big companies had the money and equipment needed.

Thanks to the internet, however, there is a new way for inventors to get money and customers: crowdfunding.

People promise in advance that they will buy an invention once it comes out. The customer only pays if the invention is actually made, but because they have promised to pay, the inventor gets the money they need for their work.

GLOSSARY

3D PRINTER
A device that uses liquid plastic (or other materials such as wood or metal) to build up a three-dimensional object by printing a series of two-dimensional layers.

ARTIFICIAL INTELLIGENCE (AI)
The ability of a machine to think by itself and not just follow a program created by humans.

ASTEROID MINING
The process of extracting valuable minerals from asteroids (small rocks orbiting the sun, between the planets).

AUGMENTED REALITY (AR)
Information and/or images electronically added to a view of the real world.

BANDWIDTH
The amount of information that can be carried by a communication channel such as a fibre-optic cable or a radio signal.

BIOMETRIC SCANNING
Use of biological characteristics, such as fingerprints, voice patterns or gestures, to recognize you and confirm your identity.

BIOMIMETIC
Mimicking some aspect of an animal's biology.

BIONIC LIMBS
Prosthetic limbs which are connected to a user's nervous system, making it possible for him or her to control them directly by thought.

BIOPOLYMER
A polymer is a substance with a molecular structure consisting of many repetitions of the same arrangement of atoms. A biopolymer is such a substance occurring in living organisms, e.g. a protein or DNA.

CARBON SCRUBBING
The use of chemical "sponges" to soak up carbon dioxide from the air.

CHIP
Short for "microchip". A tiny electronic circuit, used in almost all electronic devices.

CLONING
The practice of growing an identical copy of an animal by implanting its DNA into an egg, which then develops into an adult animal.

DEVICE CONVERGENCE
The process by which jobs that used to need different devices (such as a camera to take photos, or a CD player to play music) are increasingly done by multi-purpose devices.

DIGITAL GRAFFITI
A virtual message attached to a particular object or place, which you would see in augmented reality (AR).

DNA
The genetic material that defines the characteristics an organism will have.

DRONE
A remote-controlled vehicle or robot.

ELECTRONICS
The science and technology of using small amounts of electricity to achieve an aim.

FAMILIAR
In folklore, a familiar was a demon, usually in the form of an animal, who accompanied a witch and did her bidding. Augmented reality could be used to create your own virtual familiar to act as a digital assistant.

FIBRE OPTICS
Thin, transparent fibres of glass or plastic used to carry signals in the form of light.

FOSSIL FUELS
Fuels created when the bodies of dead plants and animals compressed over millions of years to turn into coal, oil and gas.

FUEL CELL
A cell producing an electric current directly from a chemical reaction.

FUTURIST
A person who tries to predict the future.

GENETIC ENGINEERING
Alterations to the DNA of an organism, made in order to change its characteristics.

GEOENGINEERING
The practice of intentionally changing Earth's natural systems.

GLOBAL WARMING
An ongoing rise in the temperature of the Earth's atmosphere and oceans, thought to be caused by a rise in the amount of carbon dioxide (and other greenhouse gases) in the atmosphere.

GREEN ENERGY
Renewable forms of energy such as sunlight, wind, waves and heat from the ground (geothermal energy).

GREENHOUSE GAS
A gas which traps heat in the Earth's atmosphere.

HEAD-UP DISPLAY (HUD)
Navigation and radar information shown inside the visor of a fighter pilot's flight helmet.

INTERNATIONAL SPACE STATION (ISS)
The ninth space station to orbit the Earth. The ISS was built as a collaboration between five space agencies from different countries and is expected to be in use until at least 2016.

ION DRIVE
A type of rocket motor which works by ejecting ions that have been accelerated to high speed by an electric field.

KITESHIP
A vessel fitted with a giant kite or skysail that can be winched back in and folded away when the wind is not blowing.

LIGHTCRAFT
A spaceship propelled by external lasers.

MAG-LEV (MAGNETIC LEVITATION) TRAIN
A train which uses electromagnets to generate strong magnetic forces that allow it to hover above rails without touching them.

MASER
A microwave laser. Microwaves are electromagnetic waves with a wavelength between radio waves and infrared radiation.

NANOBOT
A tiny machine, built possibly only from a few molecules or atoms.

NANOTECHNOLOGY
Technology operating on an extremely small scale, possibly manipulating individual atoms and molecules.

NEAR-FIELD COMMUNICATION
A technology which allows two electronic devices to communicate at short range.

NUCLEAR FUSION
A nuclear reaction that occurs when the nuclei of two or more atoms combine.

OCEAN SEEDING
A type of geoengineering in which iron filings are used as a fertilizer for ocean algae. The algae soak up lots of CO_2 from the air before dying and sinking, taking the carbon with them.

PERSONAL DIGITAL ASSISTANT
A device which uses apps to do tasks for you, such as controlling the heating in your home or monitoring door alarms.

PHOTOSYNTHESIS
A process used by plants to convert energy from sunlight into foods for growth.

POWER SUIT
A bodysuit made from metal, carbon fibre and other strong, light materials. It acts like an external skeleton and can be used to boost the wearer's strength and endurance.

QUANTUM COMPUTING
Computing that uses subatomic particles to carry out more than one calculation at a time and so vastly increase processing power.

RADIO FREQUENCY IDENTIFICATION (RFID)
A technology which attaches information to an object, such as a product on sale in a shop, using an RFID tag which can be read with an RFID reader.

ROADABLE AIRCRAFT
A type of small road vehicle that can be turned into an aeroplane by attaching wings and a tail section.

SOLAR PANEL
A panel made of photovoltaic cells, which convert sunlight into electricity.

SPACE ELEVATOR
A project that aims to use a thin but incredibly strong cable to run a lift from Earth to an orbiting space station, providing a permanent bridge into space.

SUBATOMIC PARTICLE
A particle that is smaller than an atom (e.g. a neutron).

SURVEILLANCE STATE
A country whose government closely monitors all inhabitants and visitors.

TELEMEDICINE
The application of telepresence to medicine.

TELEPRESENCE
The use of virtual reality technology to create the sensation of being elsewhere. It can be used for the remote control of machinery.

TELEROBOTICS
The process of controlling a robot from a distance.

TOKOMAK REACTOR
A nuclear reactor that heats plasma by blasting it with microwaves and beams of particles travelling at close to the speed of light, and then uses massive magnetic fields to crush it until fusion is achieved.

TRANSISTOR
A device used to control the flow of electricity in electronic equipment.

UNMANNED AIR VEHICLE (UAV)
A radio-controlled small aircraft such as the Predator drones used by US military forces.

THIS IS A CARLTON BOOK

© Carlton Books Limited 2014

Senior Editor: Anna Bowles
Senior Art Editor: Emily Clarke
Designer: Ceri Hurst
Production: Dawn Cameron

Published in 2014 by Carlton Books Limited

An imprint of Carlton Publishing Group

20 Mortimer Street, London, W1T, 3JW

A catalogue for this book is available from the British Library.

ISBN: 978-1-78097-322-7

Printed in China

The publishers would like to thank the following sources for their kind permission to reproduce the pictures in this book.
Key. t = top, b = bottom, l = left, r = right & c = centre

Avinc.com: 57b. Airbus: 46c, 46b, 46-47. Alamy: /EPA European Pressphoto Agency B.V: 76-77t. Aurora Spacelines: 55b. Bg Shipping: 52b. Benoit Patterlini: noart1999.blogspot.fr: 2-3, 53t. Bigelow Aerospace: 69. Boston Dynamics: 17br. Carlton Books: 22-23. Cisco Systems: 20-12. Corbis: /Adrian Bradshaw/EPA: 31br, /Aristide Economopoulos/Star Ledger: 65tr, /Peter Ginter/Science Faction: 36-37c, 37br, /Pascal Goetgheluck: 78-79, /Steffen Jahn/dpa: 44-45, /James Leynse: 15br, / Tomas Rodriguez: 21b, /Science Picture Co: 58-59, Ingo Wagner/dpa: 9tr. D Wave: 14b. Deep Space Industries: 74-75c, 75b. Eksobionics.com: 13t, 13r. Electrolux: 27t. Festo.com: 16 (all images), 17tl, 17l. First Warning Systems: 28br. Foster and Partners: 79br. Georgia Tech: 11b. Getty: 62bv, /AFP: 5, 9b, 15t, 23br, /Colin Anderson: 34-35, /Boston Globe: 11t. Google: 22. Horizon Fuel Cell Technologies: 44l. Jeff Allen Case: 50tr, 51tl. Makerbot: 21r, 78bl. Memoto: 25r. Mist-er.com: 33t. MIT: /Marcelo Coelho: 26r. Motorola: 15l. NASA: 6, 8, 10-11, 12r, 36t, 54-54c, 68bl. Nike: 21l. Nokia: 24-25. Northropgrumman.com: 56t, 56r. Paolo Venturella + MenoMenopiu Architects: 40-41. Photoshot: 12l. Planetary Resources: 75t. Press Association Images: Shizuo Kambayashi/AP: 29t. Prof Mark Cutkosky & Sangbae Kim: 26l. Rensselaer Polytechnic Institute: 54bl, 54br. Rex Features: 73t, 73r, / Isopix: 26-27c. Reuters: Francois Lenoir: 65tl. RSLSteeper: 63r. Seaorbiter.com: 53b. Science Photo Library: 13l, 17r, /BSIP, Benoist Boissonet: 9tl, Christian Darkin: 64, /Eye of Science: 16, /Chris Hellier: 39t, /Matteis/Look at Sciences: 43t, /B Murton/Southampton Oceanography Centre: 76b, /Ocean Power Deliveries/Look at Sciences: 38b, /Richard Kail: 4-5t, 14r, /Ria Novosti: 62tr, /Phillipe Psaila: 57c, 63t, /Herbert Raguet/Loot at Sciences: 57t, /US Department of Energy: 37t, /Victor Habbik Visions: 42-43c, 60-61c, 66-67, 74br, /Volker Steger: 29l. SpaceX.com: 68r. Terrafugia: 4b, 50bl, 50br. Thinkstockphotos.co.uk: 1, 30, 38t, 39b, 45b, 47t, 48-49, 51b, 65br. Topfoto.co.uk: 45t. Tubularrail.com: 33bl. Virgin Galactic: 70-71, 72-73c, 73b. Wireimage: 32

Every effort has been made to acknowledge correctly and contact the source and/or copyright holder of each picture and Carlton Books Limited apologises for any unintentional errors or omissions, which will be corrected in future editions of this book.